Wonder Writers

Teacher's Writing Resource  1

Wonder Writers: **Teacher's Writing Resource — Grade 1**

Published in the United States by Rigby
a division of Reed Elsevier Inc.
1000 Hart Road
Barrington, IL 60010-2626
800-822-8661

05 04 03 02 01
10 9 8 7 6 5

Printed in the United States

ISBN 0-7635-6933-X

Visit Rigby on the World Wide Web at http://www.rigby.com

Rigby

Table of Contents

Introduction 5

About the Mini-lessons 6

About the Writing Strategy Cards 12

Writing in a Balanced Literacy Classroom 16

    Using Read-Alouds and Think-Alouds
as Models 17

    Using Modeled Writing 17

    Using Language Experience 18

    Using Shared Writing and
Interactive Writing 18

    Using Guided Writing 19

    Using Independent Writing 20

Assessing and Planning Instruction 21

    Writing and Spelling Development 21

    "Snapshots" of Young Writers 24

    Stages of English Language Development
and Suggested Teaching Strategies 26

Mini-lessons for Grade 1 29

    Think! Think! Think! 30

    1: What Is an Author? 30

    2: Why Do People Write? 31

    3: Where Do We See Writing? 32

    4: Where Do I Write? 33

    5: Making a Class Idea List 34

    6: Making an Individual Idea List 35

    7: Flip and Accordion Books 36

    8: Alphabet, Number, and Color Books . . . 37

Let's Get Started 38

    9: Putting Your Name on Your Paper 38

    10: Copying Environmental Print 39

    11: Directionality 40

    12: Letters and Words 41

    13: Invented/Developmental Spelling 42

    14: One-to-One Correspondence 43

    15: Capitalization: First Names and "I" 44

    16: Simple Sentences 45

    17: Punctuation: Question Mark 46

    18: Punctuation: Exclamation Point 47

    19: Punctuation: Quotation Marks 48

    20: Punctuation: Commas in a Series 49

    21: Naming Words 50

    22: Action Words 51

    23: Describing Words 52

    24: Contractions 53

    25: Writing a Story (Narrative) 54

    26: Organizing Your Writing 55

    27: How to Start Your Story 56

    28: How to End Your Story 57

    29: Writing About a Picture 58

    30: Writing a Long Story 59

    31: Writing Letters and Cards 60

    32: Writing a New Adventure for a
Character 61

33: Adding on to Familiar Poems and Songs 62

34: Retelling Favorite Stories and Poems ... 63

35: Writing Nonfiction 64

36: Interviewing 65

37: Writing from Patterned Text 66

38: Writing a How-to 67

Making It Better (Content) 68

39: Reading Your Work to Yourself 68

40: Reading to a Peer or Group 69

41: Listening and Asking Questions 70

42: Asking for Comments 71

43: Conferencing with the Teacher 72

44: Conferencing with Peers 73

45: What's Important, What's Not 74

46: Adding Details 75

Making It Better (Mechanics) 76

47: Proofreading Symbols: Caret, Delete Line 76

48: Proofreading Symbols: Uppercase and
    Lowercase Letters, Punctuation 77

49: Checking Capitalization and Punctuation 78

50: Checking Spelling 79

51: Checking Sequence 80

52: Checking Word Order 81

53: Matching Words and Pictures 82

I'm an Author 83

54: To Publish or Not to Publish 83

55: Publishing 84

56: Choosing a Title 85

57: Writing a Dedication 86

58: Finishing Illustrations and Labels 87

59: Making a Cover/Binding 88

60: Author's Chair 89

61: Sharing Your Work at Home 90

Assessment 91

62: Self-Assessment (Pictorial) 91

63: Self-Assessment (Text) 92

64: Keeping Track of What You've Written . . 93

Assessment Forms **94**

Writing Checklist 94

A Bibliography of Professional Resources **96**

Introduction

Writing, like reading, is a meaning-making process. As writers compose, they think about what they want to write, write their ideas, and speak their thoughts. They read their writing and revise it to shape their ideas and find their own voices as authors. Children engaged in authentic writing experiences within balanced literacy approaches learn how to write and how to be writers who naturally and comfortably use the writing process.

Wonder Writers was developed to support teachers as they teach writing and to encourage children to want to write. *Wonder Writers* for Grade 1 is comprised of this *Teacher's Writing Resource,* which includes 64 Writing Mini-lessons, and 30 Writing Strategy Cards. *Wonder Writers* provides lessons and writing activities that engage children as they learn the skills, strategies, and techniques of "real" writers.

The *Teacher's Writing Resource* carefully outlines the design, content, and process of the Writing Mini-lessons and Writing Strategy Cards and shows you how they can both be woven easily into the balanced literacy practices in your classroom.

- The developmentally appropriate Writing Mini-lessons are designed to let you model and teach the writing process as children are engaged as real writers.

- The Writing Strategy Cards guide your classroom exploration of the strategies, techniques, and behaviors of writers.

- Children will make important reading and writing connections through the literacy experiences provided by both sets of materials.

With *Wonder Writers*, you will grow as a more reflective and effective teacher of writing while your children grow as writers.

About the Mini-lessons

By learning the procedures, techniques, and skills that writers use during the writing process, children learn to make decisions about their writing as "real authors." The *Wonder Writers* Mini-lessons are organized according to the steps of the writing process. As you can see in the chart below, these closely mirror the tasks and behaviors readers use before, during, and after reading.

Readers	Writers
Setting the Scene • activate and build prior knowledge • select topics and genre • determine purpose • consider audience of text	*Think! Think! Think!* • activate and build prior knowledge • select topics and genre • determine purpose • consider audience
Reading the Text • practice skills/strategies to read words • use strategies to create meaning • monitor meaning • use sensory images • build a flow of meaning	*Let's Get Started* • practice skills/strategies to transcribe words • use strategies to create meaning • monitor meaning • express sensory images • create a flow of ideas
Returning to the Text • ask questions • revisit text to revise meaning • strive for accuracy • focus on features of text • reflect to personalize text	*Making It Better* • ask questions • revisit text to clearly convey meaning • strive for accuracy • return to text to examine features • reflect to personalize text
Responding to the Text • go beyond text to extend learning • share their responses • value the literature • express their voices • feel success • want to reread the literature	*I'm an Author* • create a text which extends their thinking • share their writing • value their own compositions • establish their voices • feel success • want to reread their writing

Each of the 64 Mini-lessons has a clearly defined focus and a supportive teaching sequence. You may choose to present two lessons weekly or select specific lessons as needed to meet the needs of the young writers in your classroom. The Mini-lessons may be presented in small groups or with the whole class.

Step of the Writing Process

The mini-lessons are organized in five sections that follow the steps of the writing process. See pages 10 and 11 for further explanation.

Let's Get Started

Describing Words

You Will Need

On chart paper, write a short paragraph describing something. Use lots of descriptive words. For example, "Today I wore my favorite red sweater to school. I love my warm, woolly, red sweater. I like to wear it with my old, faded jeans."

Lesson Background

Through read-alouds, children hear descriptive language but have not yet made the transition to using it in their own writing. Now is the time to begin calling children's attention to the use of descriptive words in their writing.

Lesson Background

Discusses the writing development of Grade 1 children and explains the purpose of the lesson.

Teaching the Lesson

1. Read your descriptive paragraph to children. Ask them to listen for words you use that describe. As you read, be sure to emphasize the descriptive words.

2. Ask children to talk about what you described. How did they know what your clothing looked like? When a child mentions one of the descriptive adjectives in the story, circle it. After the descriptive words are circled, talk about how important it is for authors to use these kinds of words that help readers picture things in their heads.

3. Share a descriptive selection from a classroom book. Ask children to close their eyes and imagine the scene in their minds. Talk about the words the author used to help them do that. Some examples are *I Went Walking* by Sue Williams and *If You Were a Writer* by Joan Lowery Nixon.

4. Encourage children to reread a piece of their writing and find a place where they could add descriptive words. Suggest that they rewrite that section, adding the new words.

Revisiting the Lesson

Play a descriptive game. Write a sentence, using no descriptive words. Ask children to draw a picture of the subject. For instance, "The cat plays with the yarn." Have children share their pictures with a friend and talk about how they are different and why. Then write a sentence with descriptive adjectives: "The gray cat plays with the pink yarn." Now ask children to draw a picture and then compare pictures with a friend. Talk about how the use of descriptive words helped children form more precise mental images of the idea you were trying to convey.

Assessment Connection

When looking through children's writing, make a note of those children who attempt to use descriptive words in their writing. For those having difficulty, you may wish to play Twenty Questions in a small group. Stress the use of descriptive details to reveal the mystery object.

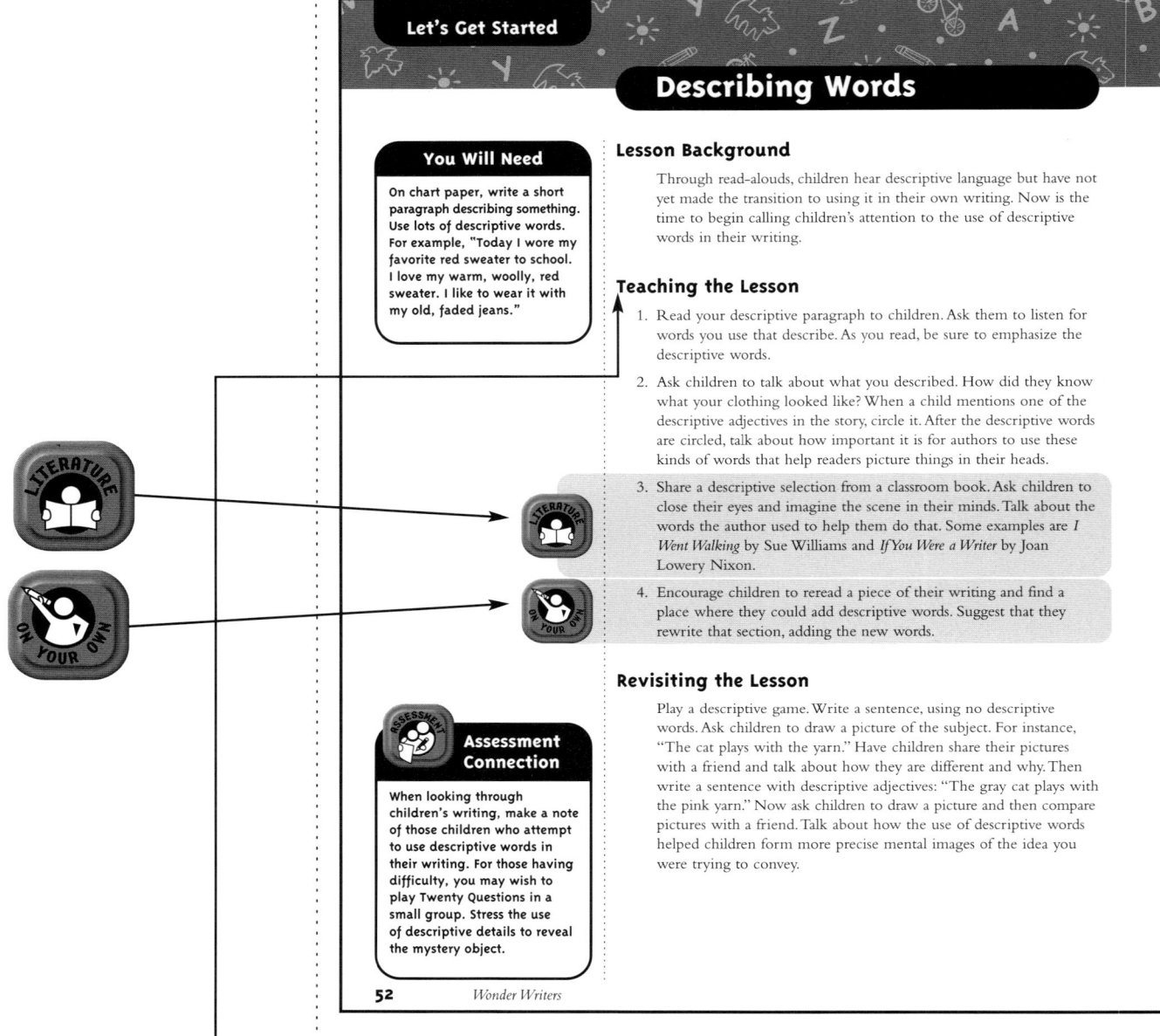

Let's Get Started

Describing Words

You Will Need

On chart paper, write a short paragraph describing something. Use lots of descriptive words. For example, "Today I wore my favorite red sweater to school. I love my warm, woolly, red sweater. I like to wear it with my old, faded jeans."

Lesson Background

Through read-alouds, children hear descriptive language but have not yet made the transition to using it in their own writing. Now is the time to begin calling children's attention to the use of descriptive words in their writing.

Teaching the Lesson

1. Read your descriptive paragraph to children. Ask them to listen for words you use that describe. As you read, be sure to emphasize the descriptive words.

2. Ask children to talk about what you described. How did they know what your clothing looked like? When a child mentions one of the descriptive adjectives in the story, circle it. After the descriptive words are circled, talk about how important it is for authors to use these kinds of words that help readers picture things in their heads.

3. Share a descriptive selection from a classroom book. Ask children to close their eyes and imagine the scene in their minds. Talk about the words the author used to help them do that. Some examples are *I Went Walking* by Sue Williams and *If You Were a Writer* by Joan Lowery Nixon.

4. Encourage children to reread a piece of their writing and find a place where they could add descriptive words. Suggest that they rewrite that section, adding the new words.

Revisiting the Lesson

Play a descriptive game. Write a sentence, using no descriptive words. Ask children to draw a picture of the subject. For instance, "The cat plays with the yarn." Have children share their pictures with a friend and talk about how they are different and why. Then write a sentence with descriptive adjectives: "The gray cat plays with the pink yarn." Now ask children to draw a picture and then compare pictures with a friend. Talk about how the use of descriptive words helped children form more precise mental images of the idea you were trying to convey.

Assessment Connection

When looking through children's writing, make a note of those children who attempt to use descriptive words in their writing. For those having difficulty, you may wish to play Twenty Questions in a small group. Stress the use of descriptive details to reveal the mystery object.

52   *Wonder Writers*

Teaching the Lesson

Your role as teacher is to invite and support your children as they share in a common writing experience as clearly defined in each lesson. Suggestions for beginning the lesson may include discussing an author, sharing writing samples, and/or explaining a writing skill, strategy, or technique. A ***Literature*** icon indicates where books are used as writing models to foster the reading and writing connection. The detailed Mini-lessons provide explicit suggestions for modeling, questioning, and encouraging children to share their thoughts about each step of writing. An ***On Your Own*** icon indicates a connection to link the content of the Mini-lesson with children's independent writing.

Let's Get Started

Describing Words

You Will Need

On chart paper, write a short paragraph describing something. Use lots of descriptive words. For example, "Today I wore my favorite red sweater to school. I love my warm, woolly, red sweater. I like to wear it with my old, faded jeans."

Lesson Background

Through read-alouds, children hear descriptive language but have not yet made the transition to using it in their own writing. Now is the time to begin calling children's attention to the use of descriptive words in their writing.

Teaching the Lesson

1. Read your descriptive paragraph to children. Ask them to listen for words you use that describe. As you read, be sure to emphasize the descriptive words.

2. Ask children to talk about what you described. How did they know what your clothing looked like? When a child mentions one of the descriptive adjectives in the story, circle it. After the descriptive words are circled, talk about how important it is for authors to use these kinds of words that help readers picture things in their heads.

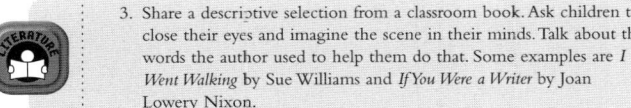

3. Share a descriptive selection from a classroom book. Ask children to close their eyes and imagine the scene in their minds. Talk about the words the author used to help them do that. Some examples are *I Went Walking* by Sue Williams and *If You Were a Writer* by Joan Lowery Nixon.

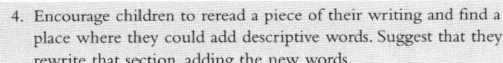

4. Encourage children to reread a piece of their writing and find a place where they could add descriptive words. Suggest that they rewrite that section, adding the new words.

Revisiting the Lesson

Play a descriptive game. Write a sentence, using no descriptive words. Ask children to draw a picture of the subject. For instance, "The cat plays with the yarn." Have children share their pictures with a friend and talk about how they are different and why. Then write a sentence with descriptive adjectives: "The gray cat plays with the pink yarn." Now ask children to draw a picture and then compare pictures with a friend. Talk about how the use of descriptive words helped children form more precise mental images of the idea you were trying to convey.

Assessment Connection

When looking through children's writing, make a note of those children who attempt to use descriptive words in their writing. For those having difficulty, you may wish to play Twenty Questions in a small group. Stress the use of descriptive details to reveal the mystery object.

52   *Wonder Writers*

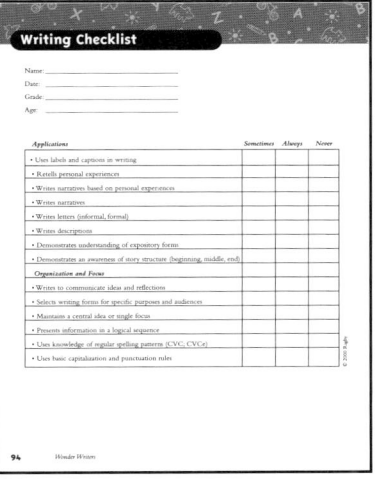

Revisiting the Lesson

The writing skills, strategies, and techniques that are introduced in the *Teaching the Lesson* section are reinforced to ensure that children retain and apply their learning when they write independently. Ideas for revisiting the lesson in future sessions are included along with additional practice.

Assessment Connection

This section highlights specific skills and strategies for evaluating children's writing samples and behavior during the lessons. Two writing assessment forms are provided on pages 94 and 95 of this guide for more formal assessment.

Wonder Writers Mini-lessons show you how to model techniques that will help children manage their writing both creatively and logistically.

Think! Think! Think! (Prewriting)

Writers have to think when they plan their writing. During prewriting, writers generate ideas, decide on a topic, determine their writing purpose, and consider the audience for their writing. Writers select the genre and format of their writing pieces. With the *Think! Think! Think!* prewriting Mini-lessons, children learn how to make these prewriting decisions as developmentally appropriate to their grade level.

Children explore different techniques for generating ideas based on their own lives, the literature they read, and their observations of the world. They plan for writing and practice ways to organize their ideas on paper. Children should be invited to venture into many different kinds of writing and to choose new formats for writing. As you honor children's choices, they will take ownership of their writing from the beginning of the writing process.

Let's Get Started (Drafting)

Writers develop their own unique ways of getting started on a writing project. They bring their interests, knowledge of chosen topics, experiences with written language, and reading experiences to the process. As they begin writing, they also learn what else they may need to find out about the topic, the structures and conventions of written language, and the features of the genres and formats in which they are planning to write.

During the *Let's Get Started* Mini-lessons, children learn to view drafting as a way to get started, a time to focus on thoughts and ideas, and a safe place to learn about written language. To guide children as they begin to draft, these Mini-lessons introduce the logistics of writing as well as creative concepts.

By observing and conferencing with children as they are drafting, you will be able to identify relevant learning needs and select from Mini-lessons that teach appropriate capitalization, punctuation, spelling, and grammar skills. As children move further into their writing projects, these Mini-lessons help them organize and develop the flow of their ideas. The draft becomes a real working copy, not just a "step" in the writing process.

The *Wonder Writers* Mini-lessons are organized into five sections according to the steps of the writing process.

See pages 30–37 for the **Think! Think! Think!** Mini-lessons.

See pages 38–67 for the **Let's Get Started** Mini-lessons.

Making It Better (Revising)

Writers learn as they read, share, and evaluate their writing. They ask themselves questions as they review and revise their pieces. Writers take time to reflect on the content of the message they are working hard to communicate. They also read for clarity and accuracy, and to make sure others can understand their writing, too. Writers need time to share, ask questions, and process responses as they work with their peers and with you.

The **Wonder Writers** *Making It Better* Mini-lessons for *Content* help children learn how to solicit input from others and to look critically at their own writing. Children share their works-in-progress with a peer or a group, listening to each other and asking questions of one another. With the Mini-lessons, children focus on editing for content to make their writing richer and clearer, which will ultimately help them find their own voices as writers.

See pages 68–75 for the **Making It Better (Content)** Mini-lessons.

The *Making It Better* Mini-lessons for *Mechanics* direct children as they edit their work for specific capitalization and punctuation skills, sentence structure, and spelling. As children read, reflect, and share, they realize the power revision has to improve their writing and empower them as individuals with valuable ideas worth sharing and preserving.

See pages 76–82 for the **Making It Better (Mechanics)** Mini-lessons.

I'm an Author (Publishing)

The *I'm an Author* Mini-lessons invite young writers to become contributing members of the literacy community in your classroom and beyond. Children review their own pieces to decide if they want to publish and how they want to publish. After writers choose the pieces they want to publish, they polish their work and craft a finished product. Sharing a finished piece becomes a celebration for the author and for the classroom.

See pages 83–90 for the **I'm an Author** Mini-lessons.

Assessment

If children are truly to view themselves as writers, it is important that they monitor their own progress. This makes them conscious of their successes and invested in improving their skills. These practical suggestions help children take ownership of their writing and strive for independence as writers.

See pages 91–93 for the **Assessment** Mini-lessons.

About the Writing Strategy Cards

The **Wonder Writers** Writing Strategy Cards are a unique and exciting innovation in writing instruction. In the past, most writing instruction has focused on the nuts and bolts of writing: rules for grammar, usage, and mechanics. A great deal of effort has also been applied to the prewriting phase of brainstorming for topics. Aside from these popular areas of focus, however, very little attention has been paid to an important part of writing success—understanding how successful writers think.

Failing to attend to writing as a meaning-making process is like teaching reading without ever discussing comprehension. The Writing Strategy Cards take children to that next level in their writing.

	Language Acquisition	Reading	Writing
Surface Comprehension	Understanding how it works	Phonics, sight words, print conventions, genres, literal comprehension, etc.	*Mini-lessons*: writing process, mechanics, print conventions, etc.
Deep Comprehension	Understanding how it connects to our experiences and connects us to the world	Read–alouds, class discussion, writing response activities, personal interpretation	*Strategy Cards*: what do other writers do, what can I do

The Writing Strategy Cards help children learn to think like writers and see themselves as writers. The 30 cards at the Grade 1 level serve as a resource for the children and for you, highlighting real-world connections to specific strategies used by all writers, regardless of experience or expertise.

The Writing Strategy Cards are organized under five broad categories: *Writers Write What They Know; Writers Collect Words, Ideas, and Other Things; Writers Don't Give Up; Writers Write for Many Reasons;* and *Writers Like to Learn.* The cards can be taught in any order. You are encouraged to use them as appropriate to meet the needs of the children in your classroom.

Writers Write What They Know

- Writers write about people.
- Writers write about things they do.
- Writers write about their everyday lives.
- Writers write about special times.
- Writers write about favorite things.
- Writers write about places they've been.
- Writers write about their feelings.
- Writers write about what they've learned.

> Writers tap into their own worlds to discover their topics and establish ownership for their compositions.

Writers Collect Words, Ideas, and Other Things

- Writers use lots of words.
- Writers read everything.
- Writers keep a notebook.
- Writers uses their senses.
- Writers write anytime they get an idea.
- Writers connect ideas.
- Writers collect facts.

> Writers make connections between their reading, their writing, and their lives. They discover their passions as they connect and collect.

> Writers solve problems and learn from their revisions as they craft their work. They understand that writing doesn't have to be perfect and that rethinking their writing is part of the process.

Writers Don't Give Up

- Writers ask questions.
- Writers read their writing.
- Writers help each other.
- Writers make mistakes.

Writers Write for Many Reasons

- Writers write alone, with a buddy, or in a group.
- Writers tell a story.
- Writers share information.
- Writers describe things.
- Writers have to remember.
- Writers want to remember.
- Writers persuade.

> Writers explore their craft and their world as they write for different purposes and for different audiences.

Writers Like to Learn

- Writers are curious.
- Writers daydream and imagine.
- Writers learn from other writers.
- Writers try new kinds of writing.

> Writers explore, research, and imagine to create their pieces. They know that they learn when they read and write.

Writers write about what they've learned.

I went to the aquarium.

Writers Write What They Know

Category
The Writing Strategy Cards are organized into five categories.

The front of each Writing Strategy Card showcases a single writing strategy and illustrates this strategy in use by young writers in an authentic experience. The front of each Writing Strategy Card is designed to be presented to children during a lesson to initiate discussion, and later displayed in a writing center on a bulletin board or on a classroom wall as an ongoing reminder and prompt.

Making the Connection presents tips for using each card as a springboard for whole-class or small-group discussion of the featured strategy.

Connecting to Real Life shows how the strategy is relevant to real-life writing examples familiar to children.

Connecting to Your Writing invites children to practice the strategy on their own.

Just for You addresses teachers as writers, with insightful, reflective questions and interesting information about authors and writing.

Writers write about what they've learned.

Rigby Literacy

Writers write about new things they have learned. They can delve into any subject that interests them. It can be a topic in science, the arts, or sports. Sometimes, writers want to write about what they've learned from personal experience. They might write what they've learned in their daily lives, from their travels, or from people they know.

Making the Connection

- Discuss the illustration on the front of the card. Read what the boy has written. Talk about where he went and what he has learned.
- Talk about why the boy is writing. Get children to realize that writing helps people to remember or to share things they have learned.
- Invite children to tell about things they have learned and might write about. Make a list or word wall of their suggestions. Include things they have learned about in school and outside of school.

Connecting to Real Life

- Share with children notes, papers, or photos that tell about something you have learned.
- Bring in examples of something you have learned, perhaps something you have made or collected. If possible, share a recipe, how-to instructions, or explanations you have written.
- Ask children to review their journals or folders and share their writing examples about something they have learned.

LITERATURE
- Show several nonfiction books such as Gail Gibbons's *Catch the Wind!: All About Kites* (Little, Brown & Co., 1995) and *Nature's Green Umbrella: Tropical Rain Forests* (William Morrow & Co., 1994) or Seymour Simon's *Bones* (Morrow Junior, 1998). Explain that authors need to learn about a topic before they can write a book on it.

Connecting to Your Writing

- Read aloud a nonfiction book by one of the authors just named. Then write notes on chart paper as children tell what they learned from the book.
- Take a walk around the school. Have children write a sentence or more about something new they learned.
- Have children write a note to their families telling about something they recently learned in school.
- Using a very simple example as a model, have children write a nonfiction book on a topic of their choice. If you made a word wall of topics earlier, refer to that to make sure everyone has something to write about. Allow time for children to research their topics and then time to share their books.

Just for You

Read about something that you have always wanted to learn more about, or write your own article or essay about something you have learned. You may want to share a lesson or teaching method that worked particularly well with your class.

©2000 Rigby Illustrated by: Claude Martinot Photographed by: Nancy Sheehan Photography

Writers Write What They Know

The back of each Writing Strategy Card helps the teacher define the featured writing strategy and provides suggestions for reinforcing the strategy with children. The back of each card provides notes for the teacher and is not intended to be read by children. As children practice each strategy, they will learn about themselves as writers and understand how to connect the strategy to their own writing. The activities are carefully designed to move gradually, the instructional focus from the card to real-world writing.

Writing in a Balanced Literacy Classroom

In a balanced literacy Grade 1 classroom, built upon a supportive learning environment, children read, write, speak, listen, and observe through authentic literacy experiences:

• The diverse lives, personalities, and learning needs of each child are valued and respected.

• Children are immersed in many types of books and print.

• All children are viewed as learners and view themselves as learners.

• Children learn to read, write, and work together as well as individually.

• There is time for practicing, sharing, and responding.

• Children's voices are heard as they make reading and writing choices and take steps toward becoming independent learners.

Wonder Writers is designed to engage children and teachers in real-life writing experiences within balanced literacy. The developmentally appropriate Grade 1 Mini-lessons and Writing Strategy Cards are built upon the strengths of learners at this grade level and are designed to accommodate varying instructional levels and learning styles. Children will make important reading and writing connections through the literacy experiences provided in ***Wonder Writers***. As a reflective teacher, you are encouraged to model and share yourself as a writer and reader as well — ***Wonder Writers*** will show you how.

Each of the balanced literacy approaches — *modeled, shared, guided,* and *independent* — involve different degrees of learner responsibility and teacher support. Learning experiences are structured to occur in independent, small, and whole groups for flexibility. The reflective, skilled teacher weighs this "balance" of literacy experiences, child/teacher responsibility, and small group/whole group instruction to plan curriculum and support children as they move toward independence. Through careful observation and assessment, you can learn the unique strengths and needs of the children in your classroom, who will undoubtedly be at different stages of language development.

When you do a Mini-lesson or present a Writing Strategy Card, the instructional approach you use will depend on children's previous writing experiences, their level of literacy development, and their ability to work together cooperatively. At the beginning of the year and when introducing particularly challenging skills and strategies, you may want to use *modeled writing*. As children grow in their literacy development and as a community of writers, you may prefer to use more *shared, interactive*, and *guided writing*. Striking the right balance among the approaches may vary from group to group and from year to year. As the primary observer of children's literacy development in your classroom, the decisions for releasing responsibility must ultimately be up to you.

Using Read-Alouds and Think-Alouds as Models

Reading aloud to children models fluent reading and introduces writers to a new world of books. Writers exposed to many different kinds of books have a wider variety of models for their own future writing. *Wonder Writers* Mini-lessons and Writing Strategy Cards both suggest a variety of quality trade book titles for reading aloud. Sharing aloud your thoughts, feelings, and observations while you read and write further helps children understand the writing process. *Wonder Writers* Mini-lessons encourage you to share your thoughts with children. Think-aloud prompts are provided to help you focus on features of the text, vocabulary, author's style, text organization, sentence structure, and writing strategies.

Using Modeled Writing

In modeled writing, you demonstrate the writing process by thinking aloud while composing a text on the board or on chart paper. In this approach, you expose children to a variety of writing forms that are determined by the purpose for the writing. As you write, you show children that composing a text requires thought and presents challenges. A modeled writing session should focus on a brief piece of writing related to the learning experiences in the classroom. In *Wonder Writers*, modeled writing is used in the Mini-lessons to show children how you make decisions about content, punctuation, spelling, grammar, vocabulary, text style, and format.

Tips For Reading Aloud

- Select books that interest children.
- Always practice reading the book and doing a think-aloud before reading to children.
- Keep the read-aloud book in the classroom to help children make reading and writing connections. The book can then be conveniently used as a familiar writing model.

Teaching Tip

A Mini-lesson should only last from 10 to 20 minutes. Keep the modeled writing short and focused on the skill or strategy featured in the Mini-lesson.

Using Language Experience

A language experience story is an authentic writing activity based on the melding of children's language and their life experiences. Children share their thoughts about an experience as you correctly scribe the words on paper. The writing piece, which becomes a text for children, is readable because the language comes from children and the content is based on personal experiences. Children have ownership for the writing. Although you are modeling the writing, the responsibility for developing the content and for reading the text is released to children. In *Wonder Writers*, language experience stories are composed about common classroom experiences and used to model writing skills and strategies.

Using Shared Writing and Interactive Writing

Shared Writing

During shared writing sessions, you serve as the scribe as you work together with children to compose and then read a text. The primary responsibility for composing the text lies with children as you contribute by sharing ideas and pointing out the use of strategies. As you write, you encourage children to also share their thinking and read the text. The content of the writing may connect with a shared or guided reading experience or another classroom event. The teaching focus may include conventions of print, strategies for spelling, writing process, writing style, and text organization. In *Wonder Writers*, shared writing is used to learn about the writing process and writing strategies while exploring different types of writing.

Interactive Writing

During interactive writing, which should naturally evolve from shared writing, teacher and children interact to compose an accurate text. Unlike shared writing, children assume a more active role by holding the pen and doing the writing. You provide explicit instruction at the "teachable" moment. The text may be kept and used as a powerful sample for documenting children's writing development. Interactive writing serves as a way to explicitly teach and practice specific writing and spelling skills.

Teaching Tip

Language experience stories may be bound into classroom books or displayed on walls so children can read and reread their own writing.

Teaching Tip

To establish ownership and identify writers, have each child use a different color of pen when contributing to the text of an interactive activity.

Using Guided Writing

Guided writing is writing by children, with guidance and instruction from you. In this child-centered workshop, children work as a community of learners who support one another through sharing and responding. Although children may select their own topics, their writing pieces may also be an extension of an independent, guided, or shared reading experience. As children are writing, you may meet with individual children and confer with them about relevant writing process issues, skills, strategies, and content.

In *Wonder Writers*, guided writing is used to guide, share, respond and extend children's thinking strategies as they practice the writing process and become more independent.

A Framework for Guided Writing

Whole-Group Mini-lesson or Writing Strategy Card Lesson (10-20 minutes)

The whole class meets for a short, focused lesson, which may relate to a shared or guided reading lesson, but does not have to. The topic of the lesson is determined by the needs of children. *Wonder Writers* Mini-lessons and Writing Strategy Cards, which may relate to writing process, style, or writing conventions, provide the focus of the whole-group session.

Individual Writing and Conferences (20-30 minutes)

Children work independently on their pieces as you circulate, observe, and confer with individuals about their writing. You continue to reinforce the Mini-lesson or Writing Strategy Card content as you conference with children individually.

Whole-Group Sharing (10-15 minutes)

The class gathers together as you facilitate a whole-group sharing to listen and respond to a writer's piece and reinforce the Mini-lesson or Writing Strategy Card focus.

Using Independent Writing

Independent writing empowers writers to explore the craft of writing and is the ultimate goal of all writing instruction. Just as we teach reading to create independent, lifelong readers, we should meet the challenge of teaching writing with the same goal. The writing ideas and extensions within *Wonder Writers* Mini-lessons and Writing Strategy Cards invite children to explore new types of writing. Children may write about relevant curriculum topics and classroom learning experiences, about the books they have read, or reflective personal pieces. The skills and strategies they learn with *Wonder Writers* will increase their mastery of writing and their confidence in themselves as writers.

Assessing and Planning Instruction

Writing and Spelling Development

Young children are busy thinkers as they learn to write. They wonder about what to write about, puzzle about how to write and spell words, and question how to organize their writing. They explore the world of print as they write, draw, review, and talk about their writing to make and maintain meaning. Within the supportive literacy experiences launched by **Wonder Writers**, children learn to develop a sense of purpose for their writing, how to consider their audience, and how to express their own voices.

While children are engaged in authentic writing experiences within **Wonder Writers**, your task is to observe their use of writing strategies, skills, and behaviors. Children's writing samples provide valuable insight into their specific developmental traits. In your classroom, children may be at different stages of writing and spelling development, yet the **Wonder Writers** Mini-lessons and Writing Strategy Cards are appropriate for all children since they present strategies that all writers use and spend lifetimes perfecting.

The point of assessing writing is to discover where each individual child falls on a continuum of development. Knowing this shows you where he or she needs to move next in order to continue to grow as a writer. Building the specific instructional experiences that will take children to this next level of growth then becomes an informed, purposeful process.

The charts on the following pages show a continuum of development for writing and spelling. These charts provide five stages of development in each area. You can use these charts, the "Snapshots" of Young Writers on pages 24 and 25, the Writing Checklist on pages 94 and 95, and the assessment connections in the Mini-lessons to identify at which stage of writing and spelling the children in your classroom fall.

Stages of Writing Development

Scribble Stage
- no recognizable letters
- lines and scribbles

Writer "reads" the scribble at time of composing.

Isolated Letter Stage
- letters begin to appear
- letters and some symbols and numbers are strung together randomly
- drawings are included that help hold meaning over time

Writer has a purpose for the writing and reads back over time.

Transitional Stage
- some high-frequency words appear often at beginning of piece
- continues to use isolated letters, symbols, and numbers
- spacing of "words" appears
- drawings are included that help hold meaning over time

Writer may pass quickly through this stage.

Stylized Sentence Stage
- some sentences using known words and repetitive phrases and sentence beginnings such as "I went to the _____"
- words from environment to complete sentences
- invented spelling
- clues to enable writer to reread message after some time

Writers who stay in this stage need more instruction and practice.

Writing Stage
- conventional spelling and some invented spelling
- complete sentences to express ideas
- creativity
- voice

Writer is concerned about the expression of ideas.

Stages of Spelling Development

Precommunicative Spelling Stage
- shows developing knowledge of alphabet
- may or may not have left-to-right directionality
- may not be readable by others
- upper and lowercase letters used indiscriminately
- uses random strings of symbols, letters, or invented symbols

Semi-Phonetic Spelling Stage
- some letter–sound correspondence
- abbreviated words
- letter-names used to represent sounds
- letters to represent sounds
- word segmentation
- left-to-right directionality

Phonetic Spelling Stage
- match between all letters and all essential sounds
- left-to-right directionality
- invented spellings rather than random attempts at words
- word segmentation and spatial orientation

Transitional Spelling Stage
- vowels appear in every syllable
- correct letters in incorrect sequence
- alternative spellings for same sounds in different words
- learned words used frequently

Correct Spelling Stage
- entire word spelled correctly
- knowledge of word structures, prefixes, suffixes, contractions, and compound words
- mastery of uncommon spelling patterns
- uses large body of known words

"Snapshots" of Young Writers

Writing samples from young writers are powerful indicators of children's knowledge of written language. An analysis of writing samples gives you a "snapshot" of the child as a writer. You can see the child's stage of developmental spelling, understanding of text composition, and use of writing strategies to craft his or her writing. These snapshots of young writers capture the level of performance that is used to assess the child's writing development. Be sure to include both teacher-selected and child-selected pieces when gathering writing samples for assessment. Children should keep their own writing folders — which can be used for collecting samples at regular intervals — for routine, ongoing assessment, and opportunistically, for checking on specific skills or strategies.

Knowing what to look for in a writing sample is key to its value for assessment. This is a skill that gets better with practice and with increased knowledge about literacy development. The following are some examples of children's writing, along with ideas on assessment for each.

Assessment of literacy development:
• connects related ideas
• uses spacing between words
• understands directionality

Wonder Writers Mini-lessons should focus on:
• capitalization
• compound words
• asking for comments

Possible ***Wonder Writers*** Strategy Card: *Writers write about things they've learned.*

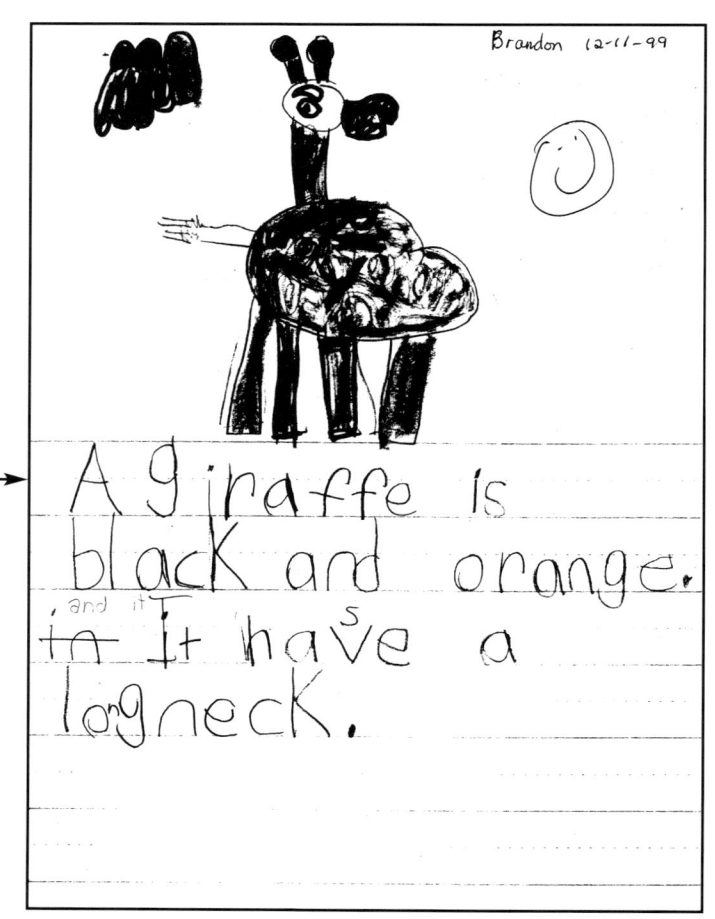

The frog 3-15-99

The frog is green.

A frog Can Swim.

A frog Can jump.

Al. A frog can Eat Flies.

I like frogs.

Ayana.

Assessment of literacy development:
- correct directionality
- maintains single focus
- uses complete sentences
- uses conventional spelling

Wonder Writers Mini-lessons should focus on:
- simple sentences
- proofreading symbols: caret, delete line
- reading your work to yourself

Possible ***Wonder Writers*** Strategy Card: *Writers share information.*

Stages of English Language Development and Suggested Teaching Strategies

When choosing Mini-lessons and Writing Strategy Cards, the following tips will provide you with help as ESL/ELL children move from stage to stage in their language acquistion and literacy development.

Stage 1: Preproduction

Children in this stage . . .
- respond primarily nonverbally
- display limited comprehension
- manipulate objects or things to communicate
- observe storytelling, shared reading, chanting, and singing
- rely heavily on pictures in shared reading

Suggested Teaching Strategies:
- Modify speech delivery by slowing down, simplifying, enunciating clearly, using gestures and body language, and supporting speech with visual aids.
- Focus primarily on group experiences.
- Lead shared writing activities that rely on picture support and focus on everyday language.
- Select activities that use real-world items children can touch, see, feel, hear, or smell.
- Follow up reading with activities that focus on drama, mime, and movement.

Stage 2: Early Production

Children in this stage . . .
- use some basic words and simple phrases
- express needs and preferences with routine language expressions
- memorize favorite rhymes, songs, and chants
- manipulate objects or things to communicate
- begin to comprehend storytelling, shared reading, chanting, and singing
- rely heavily on pictures in shared reading
- participate in guided reading only when used in a shared reading manner
- participate in language-experience situations

> *Goal: Build children's English listening comprehension and vocabulary.*

Suggested Teaching Strategies:

Use the strategies outlined for Stage 1 and add the following:

- Add group language-experience activities to your writing activities.
- Follow up reading with activities that focus on movement and drawing.
- Actively encourage children to join in a group response or repeated refrain during shared reading.

> *Goal: Continue building children's vocabulary while motivating them to produce the vocabulary they know.*

Stage 3: Speech Emergence

Children in this stage . . .

- participate in everyday conversations about familiar topics
- produce longer, complete phrases and sentences with errors that still hinder comprehension
- display increasing comprehension
- actively participate in shared reading/writing and guided reading
- rely on high-frequency words and known language patterns in shared reading
- participate in heavily scaffolded guided writing with strong teacher support
- begin to approximate independent reading

Suggested Teaching Strategies:

- Speak at a normal pace while simplifying, enunciating clearly, using gestures, and sometimes supporting speech with visual aids.
- Follow shared writing suggestions outlined for Stages 1 and 2.
- Scaffold collaborative and individual writing by providing prewriting activities that include pictures and graphic organizers like semantic webs.
- Select activities linked to, but no longer driven by, real-world items.
- Focus primarily on group experiences.

> *Goal: Continue building children's vocabulary while building higher levels of language use.*

Stage 4: Intermediate Fluency

Children in this stage . . .
- engage in ordinary conversations with more complex sentences and phrases
- make errors that no longer hinder comprehension
- begin to use multiple strategies to construct meaning from print
- actively participate in shared reading/writing, guided reading/writing, and independent reading

Suggested Teaching Strategies:
- Use normal speech, supporting academic language with visual aids.
- Incorporate interactive writing activities.
- Provide a variety of individual and group experiences.
- Engage children in meaningful discussions about books.

> *Goal: Continue building children's vocabulary and higher levels of language use in the content areas.*

Stage 5: Advanced Fluency

Children in this stage . . .
- produce language comparable to that of a native speaker
- actively use academic language to negotiate meaning
- use multiple strategies to construct meaning from print
- actively participate in all areas of balanced literacy, both reading and writing

Suggested Teaching Strategies:
- Use normal speech, supporting academic language with visual aids.

> *Goal: Continue building children's literacy learning and academic language according to grade-level expectations.*

Mini-lessons for Grade 1

The following pages contain 64 Mini-lessons organized in five sections according to the steps of the writing process. The section titles are: *Think! Think! Think!; Let's Get Started; Making It Better; I'm an Author;* and *Assessment.* See pages 10 and 11 of this guide for further explanation of these sections.

The Mini-lessons should not be taught strictly in the sequence they appear. You are encouraged to pick and choose lessons from each of the five sections as they are developmentally appropriate for the children in your classroom. For example, you will need to use lessons from the prewriting section (*Think! Think! Think!*) throughout the school year to help children find new writing topics and to encourage them to try different formats of writing. You will need to teach elements of drafting (*Let's Get Started*), revising (*Making It Better*), and publishing (*I'm an Author*) throughout the year as children work on new pieces.

Many of the Grade 1 Mini-lessons include samples of modeling think-alouds, skills, and strategies. You may want to create your own modeling passages based on personal experience using those provided as a springboard for ideas. For further information regarding the teaching of the Mini-lessons, see pages 6-9 of this guide.

Growing as Teachers and Writers . . .

With *Wonder Writers,* you will grow as a more reflective and effective writing teacher while your children grow as writers. The comprehensive and detailed lesson plans ensure that you will be teaching the skills and strategies children need. You will learn about children as individuals and about yourself as a writer as you personalize the lessons with your own writing and modeling. *Wonder Writers* invites you and your young writers to try new strategies and techniques, discover authors, and explore many types of writing and related literature. We hope both you and the children in your class will enjoy discovering the wonder of writing.

What Is an Author?

You Will Need

- several books by Steven Kellogg such as *Prehistoric Pinkerton*, *A Rose for Pinkerton*, or any of Kellogg's other tall-tale retellings
- several examples of stories published by former students

Lesson Background

As teachers, we want children to get excited about becoming authors and publishing the stories they write. We need to help children understand what this really means. This lesson is designed to give insight into one children's author, Steven Kellogg. It can be a springboard for comparison between a familiar published author and children as published authors.

Teaching the Lesson

Today we are going to meet Steven Kellogg. Does anyone know who he is? He is an author. He wrote these books. *Hold up copies of some of his books, such as* Pinkerton, Behave! *and* Johnny Appleseed. *You may want to read one of his books to the class.*

When Steven Kellogg was little, he loved animal stories and he loved to draw. Does that sound like some of you? He drew stories on paper for his younger sisters. As he drew his pictures, he told stories.

When he went to college, he studied illustration. He sent some of his ideas to publishers, people who help authors put their stories into books. They liked his ideas and started helping him make books. He has almost 90 books now.

Steven Kellogg gets ideas for his stories from many of his childhood memories. He also uses his Great Dane, Pinkerton, and his old, grouchy cat, Rose, for ideas. How might his pets have helped him get ideas for some of these books?

Many authors get ideas for writing from what happens in their lives. Anyone can write a story about something that has happened to them. When you write in class today, think of something that has happened to you that you would like to write about. Also think about Steven Kellogg and how he grew up to be an author.

Teacher Tip

Information about children's authors can be found in the library's reference section and on the Internet. Start your search by typing in "children's authors."

Revisiting the Lesson

Children need to see themselves as authors. Explain that you don't have to have a book printed by a publisher to be an author. Show several stories written by former students. Encourage children to look through the books and assure them they will all be authors too, this year.

Why Do People Write?

Lesson Background

People write for a variety of reasons, in addition to creating stories to be read for enjoyment. We want children to realize that writing is a very useful skill with many purposes.

Teaching the Lesson

1. Share with children some items you need to purchase at the grocery store. Encourage them to brainstorm how you might remember everything, concluding that making a written list would be helpful. Write your list on paper, and set it aside.

2. Explain to children that you will be using the items you buy to make something special for dinner. Show them a recipe card or a cookbook page. Tell them that this gives you the instructions for how to make the dinner.

3. Display the grocery list and recipe card. Tell children that having this information in writing will be very useful to you this evening.

4. Display a chart with the heading "Why People Write." As a group, brainstorm responses to write on the chart. Include: lists to help us remember (holiday and birthday wishes, things to do), messages to communicate (invitations, thank-you cards, birthday cards), stories to entertain (real experiences and fiction), personal feelings (memories, diaries, journals), instructions (recipes, maps, assembly instructions), labels to inform (photo albums, leftovers in the freezer), information to share (nonfiction books, newsletters, resumes), and so on.

5. Provide time for children to record two or three personal reasons for writing in their writing folder. Suggest that they choose one reason from their own list or the class list and write something for that purpose during writing workshop time.

Revisiting the Lesson

Permanently display the chart "Why People Write." Refer to it and add to it as needed. Invite children to share something from home that illustrates the various reasons people write. Have them look around the classroom to identify examples of writing. Discuss where on the chart each example could be listed. For example, names on coat hooks are labels that inform people.

You Will Need

- a recipe or cookbook
- chart paper
- marker

Teacher Tip

You may wish to explain that fairy tales were originally oral stories passed down through generations. Eventually the stories were written down so that they would not be forgotten. Gather several versions of classic fairy tales from your school library. Read aloud two versions of one story and encourage children to compare and contrast them.

Assessment Connection

Take note of the different kinds of writing each child is doing. If you have a child who is always writing lists and labels, for instance, you need to lead him or her to experiment with different kinds of writing for different purposes.

Where Do We See Writing?

Lesson Background

To function in our society we must be able to read the environmental print that surrounds us. Information, instructions, and warnings are often presented in writing. Young children should be made aware that writing is found not only in storybooks. This lesson will heighten children's awareness of environmental print and point out its importance.

Teaching the Lesson

1. After a read-aloud, discuss with children that the author told the story with written words. Storybooks, however, aren't the only place we see writing. We see written words all around us on signs, doors, in store windows—everywhere! Label a sheet of paper with the title "Writing Is Everywhere!" Explain to children that they are going to be writing detectives. (You may wish to provide each student with a paper magnifying glass for the detective work.) Have children spend three minutes searching the room for environmental print they see in places other than books. (If you have the time, you may want to take children on a walk through the school building instead.) Children should notice labels, signs, clothing, posters, advertisements, and so on, that you have placed around the room. When children return to the group, record their findings on the chart.

2. Explain to children that as authors, we can look at the writing around us for ideas and for correct spelling of words. As readers, we should pay attention to the writing we see because it may provide important and useful information.

3. Have fun discussing what might happen without environmental writing. For example, restaurants label their kitchen doors "in" and "out." Without this written reminder, the servers would risk bumping into one another. Public bathrooms are labeled "men" or "women." Just think of how embarrassing it could be if this writing were missing!

4. Invite children to create their own environmental print by labeling their desks, making personal written schedules, or adding classroom labels they feel would be helpful.

Assessment Connection

Note how well children understand and use environmental print in the classroom, such as labels for materials, class schedules, and so on.

Revisiting the Lesson

Invite children to bring examples of "Writing Is Everywhere" from home. Examples could be descriptions of environmental print to add to the chart. Or they could be actual pieces of environmental print that can be displayed around the chart.

Where Do I Write?

Lesson Background

Teachers need to provide children with appropriate places to write and to keep their writing. In this lesson, children will have the opportunity to see a variety of places where they may record their thoughts.

Teaching the Lesson

I am going to show you several places where writers keep the writing they do. When I write, I write in a journal like this one. I write about the things that happen to me during the day and about my friends and family. I write about things that I always want to remember. *Share a journal entry, or part of one, so children can begin to understand the kinds of things to include in a journal.*

Some people keep a writer's notebook. In their notebooks, they write things they have heard that caught their attention. They might write down ideas they have read about. They carry this notebook everywhere as a place to collect words. For example, in my writer's notebook I keep copies of poems that I like. I keep headlines from newspaper articles that catch my attention. I also write down things people say that I find funny or sad or interesting. For example, I have one of my favorite poems written in my writer's notebook. *Share an example from a writer's notebook, yours or a colleague's.*

One other place that writers keep their writing is in a writing folder like this. *Hold up a sample writing folder.* This is an easy way to keep your writing together.

Discuss what system of storage you want children to use. Explain to children how to keep their storage system organized.

Today when you write, use your journal (notebook/folder). You can add work to it every time you write.

Revisiting the Lesson

- As children begin to use one or more of these storage systems, revisit how to keep these storage systems organized.

- Share with children how real authors use journals, writer's notebooks, and/or writing folders as places to keep their writing. See Shelley Harwayne's *Lasting Impressions* for examples.

You Will Need

samples of the following:
- writing folder
- journal (spiral notebook)
- writer's notebook

Assessment Connection

Young children often have trouble keeping their work organized. Occasionally check their journals, notebooks, or writing folders to see if they are using them as instructed.

Making a Class Idea List

Teacher Tip

Throughout the year add additional topics to the list. Topics may be related to seasons or holidays, science, social studies, or any other curriculum or school-related area.

Lesson Background

When young children are asked to write, they may say they do not know what to write about, or they may write about the same topic over and over. It is important to help children see that a variety of topics is available. By brainstorming as a class, children can share their ideas and help each other when they get stuck.

Teaching the Lesson

Today we are going to spend a few minutes talking about things we might like to write about. When I sit down to write a story, I have to think about what I want to say. What should my story be about? Some days I have lots of ideas for stories, but other days I think and think and just cannot come up with anything I want to write about. When I can't think of an idea on my own, I need a place to find ideas. That's what we're going to do today. As a class we're going to think of all sorts of things we can write about. I will write these ideas on chart paper and we'll hang our list up on the wall so whenever any of us doesn't know what to write about, we can look at our list for help.

I often write about my family. I am going to write this on our list. I will draw a quick picture of a family next to my writing so you can remember what this word says. Who else has an idea? *Continue creating a brainstormed list of ideas. Draw simple line drawings next to the ideas to be used as picture cues for children at a later time.* Let's hang this list where we can all see it. Now when I don't know what to write about, I can read this list and maybe I will get some ideas. If you come up with other ideas later on, we can add them to our list.

Now open your journal to the last page. Use this page to make a list of your own story ideas. You can choose a few ideas from the class list, but write at least one new idea as well.

Revisiting the Lesson

If children see their teacher using the list, they will recognize its importance. As you write, either in modeled writing sessions or in your own journal, revisit the list and use it to help yourself find an idea to write about. When children say they don't know what to write about, refer them to the list or to the ideas they have recorded in their journals.

Assessment Connection

When you conference with children about their writing, ask where they got their ideas. Suggest that they add novel ideas to the class list.

Making an Individual Idea List

Lesson Background

Some children, when asked to write, cannot think of a topic. Making an "I've Got an Idea" book will provide children with a way to keep track of and organize their writing ideas.

Teaching the Lesson

1. Tell children that authors often keep lists of things that interest them or that they like to do. They can look at these lists when they need ideas for writing.

2. Explain that children are going to make their own Idea Books. Later, when they need an idea to write about, they can look in their books. Give each child an 8 1/2" x 11" sheet of paper. Show them how to fold the paper in half lengthwise, creasing the paper along the fold. Then show them how to fold the paper in half lengthwise two more times, so the creases form eight boxes when the paper is unfolded.

3. Have children put the paper on their desks with the longest fold at the top. Then have them lift the top half of the paper and cut along the creases from the open edge to the fold to form four flaps.

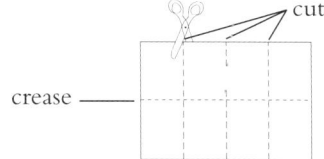 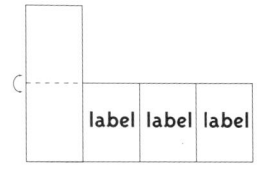

4. Once children have the flaps cut, have them label each flap with a different heading:

   Things I Do   Interesting People   Animals   Places I Go

   Explain that they can lift the flaps and write ideas that match each heading in the spaces underneath. For example, under *Animals,* they could write "My pet rabbit, Jake" or "Elephants in the jungle." Under *Places I Go,* they could write "The zoo," "Grandma's house," and so on. Later they can look at the ideas in their books when they are trying to decide what to write about. They can also add ideas to their books at any time.

Revisiting the Lesson

When children cannot think about what to write, ask them to close their eyes and look at the pictures that they see in their heads. They can make a list of all the things that flash through their minds in a minute or two of concentrating and use those ideas for writing.

You Will Need

- sample "Idea Book"
- 8 1/2" x 11" blank paper, one sheet per child
- scissors

Assessment Connection

Note children who still seem to struggle when asked to come up with an idea for writing. "Interview" these children about their interests and help them record ideas in their Idea Books or in writing notebooks.

Flip and Accordion Books

You Will Need

- a variety of trade books with unique formats, such as pop-up books, accordion books, and flip books
- supplies for making flip books and accordion books

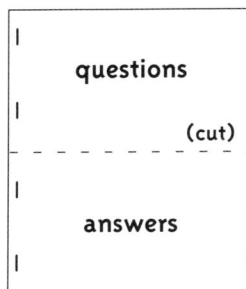

flip book

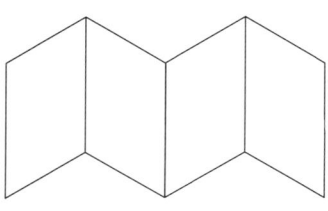

accordion book

Lesson Background

Authors may choose to present stories and factual information in a variety of interesting formats. We can help children become aware of unusual book formats, and provide opportunities for them to engage in making unique books.

Teaching the Lesson

1. Display several books with unique formats. Explain to children that in addition to writing the words for the book, the author often decides on the book's format. The format is the way in which the story or information is presented. Lead children to brainstorm why an author might choose to use a flip book or a pop-up book format. Conclude that unique book formats are visually interesting and appealing to the reader. Authors may also select a format based on the type of story or information he or she is writing.

2. Demonstrate how to make a simple flip book and accordion book. Together, discuss what kind of information or stories work especially well with these formats. For example, a flip book in which the top half and the bottom half of each page flip independently of one another is a great way to create a book used to practice skills. The top half of each page might present a question while the bottom half will provide the answer. The reader, therefore, has to flip the pages until the bottom half of the page is matched with the correct top half.

3. During independent writing time, encourage children to begin a rough draft of a story or nonfiction piece that will be formatted into a flip book or accordion book. Perhaps children could write about a current science or social studies subject. You may wish to place necessary bookmaking supplies in a center for students to use when ready.

Revisiting the Lesson

Keep bookmaking supplies on hand. As children learn new information from various curriculum areas, encourage them to create flip books, accordion books, and other books that they and their classmates can use to review what they have learned.

Teacher Tip

Celebrate children's bookmaking efforts by having them use the Author Chair to share their work. Place their books in the class library as well.

Alphabet, Number, and Color Books

Lesson Background

Authors sometimes write books to help readers acquire or practice a specific skill or concept. Many young children enjoy alphabet books, number books, and color books. We can further their interest by helping them create such books on their own.

Teaching the Lesson

1. Read aloud a few pages from each of the trade books you have gathered. Ask children how these books are similar. Discuss why the authors may have written these books. Lead children to conclude that alphabet books, number books, and color books help readers learn and practice skills. The authors have created the books for enjoyment as well as for learning.

2. If you have enough books, have children form small groups and give each group one book. Instruct the groups to look through the book together and discuss their observations about illustrations, themes, borders, and text layout. After a few minutes, have the groups trade books. Continue until every group has previewed several books. As a whole group, encourage children to share their observations about these book formats.

3. As a class, select one of the book formats discussed (or form small groups and allow each group to select a format). Assign one page for each student to create. For example, in creating an animal alphabet book, each child would complete his or her assigned alphabet page with an appropriate animal. Once all of the pages are completed, bind them together to create a class book.

Revisiting the Lesson

Continue to share appealing alphabet books, number books, and color books through shared readings and read-alouds. You may want to gather a few of these books, place them in a tote bag, and give each child a chance to take them home for several days. Include a brief letter to families about the importance of reading aloud at home, along with the day on which the tote bag is to be returned to school. It's fun to include a "comment log" so that family members may write to the class about which books they enjoyed and why. Each time the tote bag is returned, be sure to provide a few minutes for the child to share his or her family's comments.

You Will Need

one or more of each type of trade book: alphabet book, number book, and color book

Assessment Connection

As children work on pages for the alphabet book, note any difficulties they have identifying objects that begin with specific sounds or sequencing pages in order.

Putting Your Name on Your Paper

You Will Need

- a brief story you have written prior to the lesson
- two or three trade books
- chart paper

Lesson Background

Writers pay attention to both large and small details when they write. One small but important detail children often forget is to write their names and the date on their work. This is important not only for identifying authors, but for tracking a child's writing process over time. You can help children remember by explaining how important this information is and by providing a format they can follow.

Teaching the Lesson

1. Prior to the lesson, write a brief but appealing story on a piece of student writing paper. Read the story to the class with enthusiasm. When finished, explain that you want to tell the author how much you enjoyed the story. Pretend to look for the author's name on the paper. With disappointment, tell children that the author did not put his or her name on the paper. Wonder out loud, with children, "Who could have written such a wonderful story?" Conclude that you may never know.

2. Explain that to avoid being an "unknown author" children must put their names on their papers, and that adding the date tells the reader if the story was written recently or long ago. Additionally, explain that by recording the date children can look at samples of their writing over time and check their progress.

3. On chart paper or the chalkboard, model the specific format in which you want your students to write their names and the date. It is helpful to display the date each day in the same format that they will use on their paper. Explain that you will occasionally collect children's writing and that you will be unable to return it to them if a name and a date are not on the paper. As a class, decide what will happen to "unknown author" papers. Will they be placed in an "unknown author" folder? Will they be discarded? Show children where a sample of the name and date format will be permanently displayed.

4. Provide children with writing paper. Guide them as they record their names and the date as you indicate. Check their work. Then have them place the papers in their writing folders for future reference.

Revisiting the Lesson

If a student is having difficulty remembering where to write his or her name and the date, provide paper on which you have added a cue. For example, place a green dot where the name and date should begin.

Copying Environmental Print

Lesson Background

Throughout the school year, children can benefit from the development of a word wall. Interacting with the word wall through fun, brief review games is an excellent way to teach the spelling of high-frequency words, especially during the writing process. Additionally, using a word wall continually models a strategy used by good spellers—looking at environmental print.

Teaching the Lesson

1. At the bottom of each column of the class word wall, attach an envelope. (Each letter of the alphabet will have one envelope.) Label each envelope with the appropriate letter. Inside the envelopes, place high-frequency words from the word wall on individual cards.

2. Model for children how to locate the appropriate letter envelope. Children should look inside the envelope for the specific word they need, take it to their desk, and copy it into their writing folders. Stress the importance of returning the card to the correct envelope.

3. When children have copied a few words from the word wall envelopes, give them the opportunity to look for and copy words from other environmental print found in the classroom. Allow children two minutes to find and copy a word into their writing folders. Be sure to briefly check each child's word for accuracy.

4. During interactive writing, remind children to use environmental print as a spelling resource. For example, they may be unsure of how to spell the word *crayon* in their writing. Lead them to see that they can copy this word from a crayon box.

Revisiting the Lesson

Lead children in brief interactive games with the word wall. For example, play "I'm thinking of a word. . ." Tell children to search the word wall as you provide clues. Continue to narrow the list of possibilities until children locate the correct word from the word wall. Have a volunteer spell the word aloud.

You Will Need

- environmental print to display
- a class word wall

To create a word wall, high-frequency words along with other words are listed under their beginning letter. Often, a simple drawing of the word is also added. Patricia Cunningham's *Phonics They Use* details many easy and practical ideas to help create and use word walls.

Assessment Connection

As you review children's writing, notice whether or not words from the word wall and their personal word lists are being copied correctly. During individual conferencing, select one or two misspelled high-frequency words. Ask the child where he or she might find the correct spelling of the words, and encourage revision.

Directionality

You Will Need

- a familiar big book
- writing paper
- green and red crayons for each child

Assessment Connection

If some children are having difficulty with directionality, work with them individually. Have them reread a familiar piece, using their fingers to show you how they progress across and down the page.

Lesson Background

Young children, especially those with limited literacy experiences, may not use correct directionality when writing. Correct directionality is demonstrated through shared reading, along with modeled, shared, and interactive writing experiences. However, explicit instruction is also beneficial.

Teaching the Lesson

1. Using a familiar big book, point out proper directionality. This includes left to right, top to bottom, and the return sweep. Be aware that not all children know the difference between left and right. Always point as you are reading.

2. Explain that as children write, they too will need to follow this format. Provide each child with a piece of writing paper and green and red crayons. Explain that since green represents "go," we will place a green dot where writing should begin. Model this and then instruct children to do the same on their papers. Repeat this procedure using the red dot to mark the end of the line. Allow children a few minutes to write something on the marked line. They may wish to write the alphabet or begin a story. Tell them to stop writing when their pencils get close to the red dot. Once everyone has done this, ask children where they will begin writing again. Model the return sweep by running your hand under the text and down to the next blank line. Instruct children to mark this line with their green and red crayons. They may then write on this line. Continue in this manner for a few lines.

3. During independent writing time, remind children to be especially aware of their writing direction. Encourage them to use the green and red crayons on their paper if needed. You may wish to provide paper on which you have placed green dots and red dots for children who are displaying difficulty with directionality. A small arrow may also be added at the end of each line to indicate the return sweep.

Revisiting the Lesson

When involving children in interactive writing experiences (sharing the pen with children during shared writing), always discuss and model directionality. For example, you might say, "We have run out of room on this line. Who can come to the chart paper and get the next word started?"

Letters and Words

Lesson Background

Stringing letters together, apparently at random and often without spaces, is an early stage of writing development. While some children independently move on from this stage, others need explicit instruction and modeling before they can progress.

Teaching the Lesson

1. Using a shared reading approach, enjoy a familiar poem or big book with children. When finished, explain that today you want to discuss letters and words. Frame one word of text. Tell children that this is one word and that it is made up of several letters. Encourage children to count the number of letters in the word with you and then to chant each letter aloud. Explain that each of these letters is also found in other words. However, when they are grouped together in this order, they always spell this word. Repeat with several more words.

2. Frame another word, being sure this time to include the space before and after the word. Introduce your "Spaceman" tongue depressor and place it on the space before the word. Explain that to keep words from bumping into one another, writers leave a space both before and after each word. Using "Spaceman," locate several spaces while pointing out that spaces tell the reader where one word stops and another begins. Ask volunteers to come to the text, frame a word, count the number of letters, and use "Spaceman" to point out the spaces before and after.

3. Explain to children that as they write, they too will need to form words from letters and include a space before and after each word. To help them remember, provide each child with a craft stick or tongue depressor. Provide markers and encourage children to decorate their "space person." Instruct them to keep this in their writing folder to use as needed.

Revisiting the Lesson

Display a sentence that you have incorrectly copied from the shared reading text. (Be sure to exclude all spaces.) Use this to demonstrate how difficult it is for the reader to make sense of this sentence. Remind children of "Spaceman." Then use "Spaceman" as you rewrite the sentence with spaces. Read the revised sentence with children.

You Will Need

- a tool to frame words (paper frame, magnifying glass without the glass, etc.)
- "Spaceman"—a tongue depressor or wooden craft stick on which you have drawn a face
- a wooden craft stick or tongue depressor for each student

Assessment Connection

When reviewing children's writing, observe their use of spacing. Work with small groups or individuals who may require further modeling of this skill.

Invented/Developmental Spelling

You Will Need

- chart paper
- marker
- childlike t-shirt

Lesson Background

Some first graders write without hesitation, writing letters and sometimes words. Other first-grade children, when asked to write, have no idea how to go about this mysterious process. It is our job to model this process.

Teaching the Lesson

Today I have on my "first-grade t-shirt." As I write my story for you I am going to write as I might have written when I was your age. I know that when I was in first grade I had to think hard about how to spell the words in my story.

Begin to write your story on chart paper. As I write I know I have to say my words out loud and stretch them out, so I can hear the sounds better. *(Example: My dog likes to run.)* M-y ... I hear an *m. M-y* ... The next thing I hear sounds like an *i. d-o-g* ... That word begins like David's name, with a *d. d-o-g* ... When I say the next sound, my mouth makes a circle like an *o.* That sound is like the o picture name on our ABC chart, *octopus. d-o-g* ... The next sound is definitely a *g,* just like in *go. Continue in this way. When you get to* likes, *do not worry about silent letters. For the* u *in* run, *you may want to make a connection with the word* up. *(The modeling of invented/developmental spelling may be something you want to share with families, also.)*

When I write I need to go back and read what I've written. Sometimes I forget what comes next in my story. The words on the paper help me figure out what I should write next. *Be deliberate about one-to-one correspondence between the written and spoken language.*

Today, when children write, remind them to make sure they say their words aloud and stretch them out to hear the sounds. Remind them to look around the room at the charts and word wall to help with spelling some of the words. Make sure they read what they've written, too.

Assessment Connection

Using the developmental spelling stages, analyze children's writing and note one teaching point to make with each child.

Revisiting the Lesson

Ask a volunteer to share a sentence with the class that he or she would like to write. Act as the scribe, stretching out each word and having children help you hear and spell the sounds.

One-to-One Correspondence

Lesson Background

As children develop into readers and writers, they must understand that one printed word stands for each spoken word. This concept of one-to-one correspondence should be modeled frequently for children. It is crucial to their ability to comprehend what they read and to be understood when they write.

Teaching the Lesson

1. Announce that today you will be distributing new pencils (or folders, etc.) to each child to use during writing time. Tell children you have counted them out and so you know there are exactly as many pencils as there are children in the room. Then begin handing out the pencils, giving some children two or more. When you run out before getting around to each child, have the class help you figure out what went wrong. Lead children to understand that there must be an even match of one pencil to one child.

2. Point out that it is the same thing with reading and writing and words. When you read, every word on the page matches a word that you think or say. When you write, every word on your page matches a word that you think or say. Use a big book, or sample sentences on chart paper, and a pointer to illustrate. Invite volunteers to use the pointer and do the reading.

3. On chart paper, work through some examples of one-to-one correspondence in writing. Share a sentence that you want to write ("There is a dinosaur under my bed.") and then write the sentence, leaving out a few words ("There dinosaur under bed.") Let children find and help correct the errors.

4. Remind children to make sure their writing today includes all of the words they are thinking or saying. Briefly review how to check for this (pointing to words as they reread what they have written).

Revisiting the Lesson

As you read a big book, ask one child to use a pointer to point to each word that you read. Then trade roles and have the child read while you use the pointer.

You Will Need

one pencil (or eraser, folder, etc.) for each child

Assessment Connection

Watch children as they read aloud. Pointing to each word as they read is crucial at the emergent reading stage. It will also help you evaluate a child's development in the concepts of print, spacing, and one-to-one correspondence.

Capitalization: First Names and "I"

You Will Need

several sentences written on the chalkboard using childrens' names and the pronoun *I* with intended capitalization errors

Lesson Background

It is not unusual for young writers to use improper capitalization. With modeling and explicit instruction, we can help children begin to use correct capitalization for the pronoun *I* and proper names.

Teaching the Lesson

1. On the blackboard, write a simple sentence that includes your name. For example, "During the summer, Ms. Jones went to the beach." After reading the sentence aloud, explain that people do not generally refer to themselves by name. Erase your name and replace it with *I*. Read the sentence again. Explain that when the word *I* stands for a person's name, it is always capitalized, just like names are.

2. Display several previously written sentences. These sentences should include childrens' names and the pronoun *I*. Purposely include several capitalization errors. Together with children, read the sentences and correct all errors.

3. Allow children several minutes to add the names of two or three friends to their personal word lists. Remind them to start first and last names with capital letters.

Revisiting the Lesson

- Use children's surroundings to review capitalization. Provide each child with a piece of scrap paper. Explain that you are going to set a timer for three minutes. Each child should search for and copy as many names as he or she can find before the timer sounds. Encourage them to use environmental print, name tags, and trade books. Remind children to use a capital letter to begin each name. At the conclusion of the three minutes, allow time for children to share their findings.

- During shared reading and interactive writing, draw children's attention to the capitalization of *I* and proper names.

Simple Sentences

Lesson Background

Many young children do not consistently use beginning capitalization and ending punctuation in their writing. We can help them with repeated modeling and instruction.

Teaching the Lesson

1. Lead children in a shared reading of a familiar big book. Stop at the end of a page with several sentences, and ask children how a reader knows where a sentence begins and where it ends. Lead children to observe that the first word of every sentence begins with a capital letter, and that every sentence ends with some type of punctuation mark.

2. Display a sentence strip on which you have copied a simple sentence from the shared reading. Show children that the sentence you wrote matches the one in the big book. Read the sentence with children. Point out the capitalization of the first word and the period.

3. Cut your sentence strip into individual word cards, putting the period on a separate card. Distribute the cards to volunteers. Instruct children who are holding the cards to come to the front of the group, display their cards, and line up so that together they have re-created the sentence. (They may wish to look at the big book for guidance.) Encourage remaining children to read the words, deciding if their peers are standing in the correct order. Point out that the first child is holding a word that begins with a capital letter, and the last child is holding the period. If time permits, repeat with other sentences.

4. On the chalkboard, display a simple sentence such as "Playing hopscotch is fun." Remind children that the first word is capitalized and the sentence ends with a period. Then display "Playing _____ is _____." Encourage children to fill in the blank as they wish and write the entire sentence using correct capitalization and ending punctuation.

Revisiting the Lesson

Record several more sentences from the big book on separate cards. Place these, and the lesson examples, in individual envelopes. Hand out the envelopes to small groups of children. Have each group lay out its word cards to create a sentence that starts with a capital letter and ends with an ending punctuation mark.

You Will Need

- sentence strips (purchased or made from strips of oak tag)
- a familiar big book for shared reading
- a sentence copied from the big book onto a sentence strip

Assessment Connection

By monitoring a child's writing and maintaining individual checklists or anecdotal records, you will be able to track each child's mastery of this skill.

Teacher Tip

You may wish to refer to *Phonics They Use* by Patricia Cunningham for further information on "Being the Words" and similar activities.

Punctuation: Question Mark

Assessment Connection

Look through children's work to see if they are using question marks appropriately. If some children are having trouble, review this mini-lesson with them.

Lesson Background

Children must understand that different end marks in a sentence communicate different things to the reader—they indicate a statement, ask a question, or show excitement. One of the end marks that often causes beginning writers confusion is the question mark.

Teaching the Lesson

Please listen to me say two sentences. One of them will be a question and the other won't. *Say the following sentences: You are coming with me now. Are you coming with me now?* Which sentence asked a question? That's right, the second one did. The first was a telling sentence, not an asking sentence. Could you hear the question in my voice when I said the second sentence? When we ask questions, our voices go up at the end.

When we write, our readers can't hear our voices. How can we show them that a sentence is a question? Yes, we can put a question mark at the end of the sentence. Look at these two sentences. Can you tell right away which is a question? Yes, "Is it hot today?" is a question. We can see the question mark. We can hear the question when we read the sentence out loud.

On the chart paper, write the sentence "I can go home now." Read the sentence aloud to children. Is this sentence a question? No, it's a telling sentence. There is no question mark at the end. Who could change the words around to ask a question? *Help children realize that changing the word order and adding a question mark will make the sentence a question:* "Can I go home now?"

There are words that signal us that a sentence is a question. Here are some of them. *On the chart, list the following words:* who, what, where, when, why, how. Today I want you to choose one of these question words. Then write a question that starts with that word. Remember to put a question mark at the end of your sentence. Then ask a friend to read your sentence. As your friend reads, listen for a question mark in his or her voice. The question mark you write signals your friend that the sentence is a question.

Revisiting the Lesson

Occasionally take time to have children identify and reread questions they encounter in their reading and writing. Remind them to look for question marks and to read those sentences with question marks in their voices.

Punctuation: Exclamation Point

Lesson Background

While young children may tell stories enthusiastically, they may be unaware of how to translate this expression into the written form. We can help children learn that the exclamation point is a tool used by the writer to imply emotion.

Teaching the Lesson

1. Lead children in a shared reading of a familiar big book or poem. Select a sentence from the text that ends with an exclamation point, and copy the sentence onto chart paper or the chalkboard. Read the sentence aloud with appropriate intonation. Point to the exclamation point, explaining that this is sometimes used to end a sentence instead of a period. Further explain that a writer uses an exclamation point to show strong feelings. Write the sentence again, this time ending it with a period. Read the sentence as it would sound without an exclamation point. Discuss with children which of your two readings demonstrated more excitement or enthusiasm. Repeat with several sentences from the shared reading.

2. Read the short story you previously prepared. Purposely read with little expression. When finished, ask children if they think the story could be improved by including a few exclamation points. Together, add one or two exclamation points where appropriate. Read the story again with expression.

3. Have children choose a a finished or unfinished story from their writing portfolios. Ask them to evaluate the text to see if adding one or two exclamation points would be an improvement. Have them add the new punctuation marks. Ask a few volunteers to read the revised sentences aloud, with expression.

Revisiting the Lesson

Continue to point out exclamation points during shared reading and interactive writing experiences. With a child's permission, display his or her work on the overhead projector or on chart paper. Together with children, decide where an exclamation point may be added or where one should be removed.

You Will Need

- a familiar big book or poem that includes a few exclamation points
- a short story written by you to which exclamation points may be added

Teacher Tip

If children are unsure whether a period or an exclamation point should be used, reading the sentence aloud may help. If, when the sentence is read aloud, the child naturally uses enthusiasm, the sentence may require an exclamation point. If it sounds more like a "telling" sentence, a period is appropriate.

Assessment Connection

Following the introduction of exclamation points, many children temporarily overuse them. Monitor each child's writing to determine if exclamation points are being used appropriately or randomly.

Punctuation: Quotation Marks

You Will Need

- a familiar big book that includes direct speech
- sentence strips or oak tag strips

Assessment Connection

Most first-grade writers will not consistently use correct punctuation. Periodically assess each child's writing to determine whether or not the child attempts to use quotation marks and if they are being used correctly. As an individual assessment, you may wish to provide simple written sentences and ask the child to add quotation marks where appropriate.

Lesson Background

While we can introduce and expose children to quotation marks during shared reading experiences, children do not typically begin incorporating quotation marks into their writing without explicit instruction.

Teaching the Lesson

1. Using a familiar big book, point out the use of quotation marks. Explain that quotation marks are placed before and after the exact words that someone has said. Highlight a simple sentence such as *"We had a great time!" said Sammy.* Select one child to be Sammy and another child to be the narrator. Help each child read his or her part aloud to the class. Locate several more direct speech sentences and allow additional children an opportunity to read aloud. Point out that the character does not say, "he said," which is why those words are not included within the quotation marks.

2. Inform children that they may wish to add direct speech to their writing to make it more interesting and exciting. Using a sentence written on a sentence strip, clearly model how to place quotation marks before and after the words spoken. Provide each child or pair of children with a sentence written on a sentence strip. Allow them a few minutes to work on their own, reading their sentence and adding quotation marks. Ask that each sentence be placed on the chalk ledge when completed. Encourage children to read each sentence as a whole group, and decide if the quotation marks are written correctly. If they are not, call on volunteers to make corrections.

3. Ask children to include at least one "speaking" sentence with quotation marks in their journal or writing project during independent writing time.

Revisiting the Lesson

- Before reading a familiar big book, cover all quotation marks with small self-stick notes. Or, copy a poem onto chart paper with all quotation marks left out. During shared reading, invite children to replace or uncover the quotation marks.

- Children may enjoy creating quotation marks in sentences written on chart paper by gluing or taping uncooked elbow macaroni pieces in the appropriate spots.

Punctuation: Commas in a Series

Lesson Background

Most first graders are only beginning to understand the use of commas in their writing. This mini-lesson will give them practice in using commas to separate items in a series.

Teaching the Lesson

1. Show children the sentence you have written on the chart paper or board. Tell them to imagine they are going to do your shopping for you, using this list. Ask children to call out the things you need from the store.

2. Children might call out the following: soap, pickles, string beans, chips; or they might call out the items this way: soap, pickles, string, beans, chips.

3. Ask children how you could show them how many items are on your list, without rewriting it. Help them conclude that adding commas would clarify things. Explain that there are four things on your list.

4. Ask a volunteer to put a comma after each item on the list. Guide children to also see that the word *and* always appears before the last item in the series. Ask children to look through some of their favorite classroom books to find a series of items with commas. Have them count the number of items in the series.

5. Have children look through their writing folders for examples of things they've listed in a series. Have them check to see whether or not they've used commas correctly. Remind them to pay attention to their use of commas during independent writing time today.

Revisiting the Lesson

Give children an opportunity to write a sentence that includes a series of items. They could write a note about materials to bring from home for a project. Or they could make a list of children in the same row or at the same table. Any series will do as long as it has at least four items in it. Have children write the list in sentence form and use commas to separate each item. For example, "I sit at a table with Jaime, Sandy, Henry, and Tasha."

You Will Need

On a piece of chart paper or on the board, write the following sentence:

"I went to the grocery store to buy soap pickles string beans and chips."

Assessment Connection

Look for examples of commas in a series in children's writing. Ask them to clarify for you how many items are in the series. Check that commas have been used appropriately.

Naming Words

- four different colored markers or pieces of chalk
- the following words on a piece of chart paper or on the board:
  girl
  Alaska
  contest

Lesson Background

As children start to write, they should begin to understand that a sentence is made of different parts of speech, such as nouns, verbs, adjectives, and adverbs. Naming words are nouns, and in a sentence they represent a person, a place, or a thing.

Teaching the Lesson

1. Tell children that naming words, or nouns, are the words in a sentence that stand for a person, place, thing, or idea. Read the words you have written on chart paper and ask children to repeat them with you.

2. Ask a volunteer to tell you which of the words names a place. Ask that child to come up and, using one of the colored markers or pieces of chalk, draw a line under the word *Alaska*. Do the same with each of the other categories of naming words, using a different color for each.

3. Write the following sentence on the board:

   Jason has two sisters.

4. Ask a volunteer to come up and identify the naming words. Have the words underlined in the color that tells which category of naming word each belongs to. Note that there are two naming words in this sentence, and they both tell about people. They should be underlined with the same color marker or chalk.

5. Now write a few more simple sentences on the board and ask volunteers to keep coming up to the board and, using their colored markers or chalk, show you which words are naming words and whether they name people, places, or things.

6. During independent writing time, ask children to select a piece of their own writing. Working with partners, have them find and circle the naming words in their pieces.

Revisiting the Lesson

- Later, when reviewing a piece of class writing, review the concept of naming words. Ask volunteers to identify and mark naming words in the piece. Discuss what category each falls into.

- As children line up to go to recess or dismissal, ask each one to say a naming word before they take their places in line.

Action Words

Lesson Background

When children begin to write, their tendency is to use the same verbs, or action words, throughout their writing. We need to show children how using a variety of words to describe actions that can make their writing "come alive" for the reader.

Teaching the Lesson

1. Read the following sentence to children:

   Jim jumps.

2. Ask children if any of the words in the sentence describe an action. When the class agrees that the word *jumps* is an action, tell them that action words are called *verbs*. Verbs help a writer describe action.

3. Explain that you are going to give children a direction to follow. Then say, "Move your hands." After children have responded, point out how each member of the class moved his or her hands in a different way. Explain that when you used the word *move*, you did not give a specific picture of what you wanted everyone to do.

4. Now give children another direction to follow. Say, "OK, clap your hands." After they have responded, guide them to see that the verb *clap* names a specific type of hand movement, so they had a clearer picture of how you wanted them to move their hands.

5. Write a simple sentence on the board, such as "Jim goes to school every day." Ask children to identify the action word, or verb. Underline the word *goes* after children identify it. Ask them to brainstorm a list of verbs that are more specific than *goes*. Write these words on the board under the sentence. Children may suggest words such as *runs, skips, races, jogs, rides*.

6. Remind children to use a variety of verbs in their writing. They might even want to replace verbs after they've written their first draft and are preparing to "make it better."

Revisiting the Lesson

Make an action words poster to hang on the classroom wall. Brainstorm a list of specific action words, or verbs, for children to use in their writing. Add to the list as children come up with good action words.

Assessment Connection

When conferencing with children about a piece of writing, point out verbs that could be replaced with more specific words. Guide children to revise sentences using such verbs.

Describing Words

You Will Need

On chart paper, write a short paragraph describing something. Use lots of descriptive words. For example, "Today I wore my favorite red sweater to school. I love my warm, woolly, red sweater. I like to wear it with my old, faded jeans."

Lesson Background

Through read-alouds, children hear descriptive language but have not yet made the transition to using it in their own writing. Now is the time to begin calling children's attention to the use of descriptive words in their writing.

Teaching the Lesson

1. Read your descriptive paragraph to children. Ask them to listen for words you use that describe. As you read, be sure to emphasize the descriptive words.

2. Ask children to talk about what you described. How did they know what your clothing looked like? When a child mentions one of the descriptive adjectives in the story, circle it. After the descriptive words are circled, talk about how important it is for authors to use these kinds of words that help readers picture things in their heads.

3. Share a descriptive selection from a classroom book. Ask children to close their eyes and imagine the scene in their minds. Talk about the words the author used to help them do that. Some examples are *I Went Walking* by Sue Williams and *If You Were a Writer* by Joan Lowery Nixon.

4. Encourage children to reread a piece of their writing and find a place where they could add descriptive words. Suggest that they rewrite that section, adding the new words.

Revisiting the Lesson

Play a descriptive game. Write a sentence, using no descriptive words. Ask children to draw a picture of the subject. For instance, "The cat plays with the yarn." Have children share their pictures with a friend and talk about how they are different and why. Then write a sentence with descriptive adjectives: "The gray cat plays with the pink yarn." Now ask children to draw a picture and then compare pictures with a friend. Talk about how the use of descriptive words helped children form more precise mental images of the idea you were trying to convey.

Assessment Connection

When looking through children's writing, make a note of those children who attempt to use descriptive words in their writing. For those having difficulty, you may wish to play Twenty Questions in a small group. Stress the use of descriptive details to reveal the mystery object.

Contractions

Lesson Background

When we speak, we often combine certain words. These combined words are called *contractions*. Children need to understand that any word they speak they can also write, including contractions.

Teaching the Lesson

1. Ask children if they know what a shortcut is. Guide them to understand that just as we can take a shortcut to school and get there more easily and quickly, a contraction is a shortcut we use when we speak and when we write. It helps us say two words more easily and quickly.

2. Read aloud the sentences you've written on the chalkboard. Guide children to see that the second sentence in each set means exactly the same as the first, but you took a shortcut, or used a contraction, to write it.

3. Tell children that the way we write a contraction is to put an apostrophe where we have left out one or more letters. Write the contractions below on chart paper, modeling how and where to write the apostrophe. Say each word as you write it, and model using it in a sentence.

can't = cannot	don't = do not
isn't = is not	won't = will not

4. Divide the class into four groups. Assign each group one of the contractions. Ask them to spend a few minutes practicing the contractions, saying them first and then writing them. Visit each group, making sure they are putting each apostrophe in the correct place. You may also want children to use the contractions orally in sentences.

5. Remind children that using contractions can help make their writing sound more natural to the reader. Encourage them to include contractions in either the drafting or revision stage during the next writing time.

Revisiting the Lesson

Copy a short paragraph that includes contractions onto chart paper or the chalkboard. Instead of writing the contractions, write the two words. Ask volunteers to find each pair of words that can be replaced with a contraction. Ask them to draw a line through the words and write the contractions above them.

You Will Need

Write the following sentences on chart paper or on the chalkboard:

I cannot wait for lunch.
I can't wait for lunch.

I do not like spinach.
I don't like spinach.

Teaching Tip

You may wish to write the contractions in this lesson on a poster to hang on the wall for future reference, and add to it as children learn new contractions.

Writing a Story (Narrative)

Lesson Background

Getting started is often the most difficult part of the writing process. We can help children begin to write stories by first encouraging them to tell about memorable experiences. Discussing an experience will help children focus their ideas for writing.

Teaching the Lesson

1. You may want to introduce this mini-lesson by reading aloud from *Bigmama's,* by Donald Crews, or another book that tells about a shared memory.

2. With children gathered around you, show them a special memento such as a photo, an item of clothing, or a book. In a storytelling manner, share an experience that makes the item meaningful to you. Be sure to include a clearly stated beginning and ending to your story. When you are finished, encourage children to ask questions and retell their favorite parts. Relate your story to the book you shared, explaining that you shared a memory just as the author did.

3. Tell children you do not want to forget your story so you will write it on chart paper. Compose and record your story in front of children while thinking aloud. Just as you did verbally, be sure to model proper story structure, using a clear beginning and ending. When done, read the story aloud, asking children if the written version is similar to the version you told them.

4. Ask children to each recall an experience that they think they will remember for the rest of their lives. Have them draw a picture that reminds them of the experience. Ask them to write one or two sentences about the picture as well. Suggest that children save their drawings in their writing folders. Later they may want to develop a longer story about the experience.

Revisiting the Lesson

Ask each child to bring a special memento (photo, toy, trophy, etc.) to school. You may wish to inform families so that they may help their child choose something appropriate. Once everyone has a memento in school, encourage children to form small groups or partnerships. Instruct them to briefly share their items in a storytelling format. Have them ask questions and make comments only after the speaker has finished talking.

You Will Need

- a trade book that tells about a shared memory or a special memento. Suggested titles:
  Bigmama's by Donald Crews
  A Chair for My Mother by Vera B. Williams
  The Quilt Story by Tony Johnston
  Home Place by Crescent Dragonwagon
- a personal memento

Organizing Your Writing

Lesson Background

A good writer knows how to organize his or her writing so that the piece flows from beginning to middle to the end. This mini-lesson will help children develop a story by breaking it down into these three separate and distinct pieces.

Teaching the Lesson

1. Ask children to pick a partner to work with and choose something they would both like to write about.

2. Distribute the forms you made up, one to each pair. Ask children to decide how they will record their writing—one can draw the pictures and the other write the words, or they can take turns, or they may use any way they would like to work it.

3. Explain to children that they should first think through their stories and decide what will happen. Caution them to make their stories short and simple.

4. In the first box, instruct children to draw a picture of whatever happened FIRST in the story. They should then write the accompanying text for that picture. Some children may choose to write the text first and then draw the picture.

5. The middle section of the page is for the middle of the story, or what happened NEXT.

6. The last section is for the end of the story, or what happened LAST.

7. When children are satisfied with their stories, ask them to share them with the rest of the class.

8. Ask children to reread a piece of writing from their writing folders. Have them use three different colors of markers or crayons to identify the beginning, middle, and ending sections of their work.

Revisiting the Lesson

Read a short story out loud to children, asking them to listen for what happened first, next, and last. Encourage them to take notes to help them remember.

You Will Need

Make a form that looks like the one shown here. It should have three boxes on the left, big enough for children to draw pictures in, and blank lines for text at the right.

First, _____
_____

Next, _____
_____

Last, _____
_____

How to Start Your Story

Lesson Background

Beginning writers often have trouble getting started. Even when they know what they want to write about, they may struggle to get the first sentence on paper. This mini-lesson will provide some suggestions for giving classroom authors a "jump start" on their writing.

Teaching the Lesson

Sometimes the hardest part about writing is getting started. Let's see how some of these authors started their stories. *One at a time, read aloud the first few words or first sentence of several big books.*

How are these story beginnings alike? How are they different? Are they interesting? Do they make you want to know more about the story?

Let's think of some good story beginnings that we can use when we get stuck. I will start our list. *Read aloud each of the following story starters as you write:*

> Once upon a time . . .
> One dark night . . .
> After the huge snowfall . . .
> When I was very little . . .

Can anyone suggest another story starter? I will add your ideas to the list. *Record children's ideas. If they offer ideas that are very similar to some already on the list, you might want to amend suggestions. For example, "One dark night/sunny morning/rainy day..."*

Now I would like you to choose one of the story starters that interests you. Write it on a piece of writing paper. Think about a story you could tell that starts with those words. Then write a few sentences or a longer story.

Revisiting the Lesson

As you are reading children's writing throughout the year, copy down some of the story starters that you particularly like. Add these to the poster, making sure you give credit to the children who wrote them.

Assessment Connection

Note children who seem to always start their stories in the same way, or who still have trouble getting started at all. Revisit the class list of story starters with them to help them begin using it as a reference.

How to End Your Story

Lesson Background

It is often difficult for young writers to add satisfying conclusions to their writing. Instead, their stories often end abruptly. It is helpful for children to see this part of writing modeled with several examples of story endings provided.

Teaching the Lesson

1. Display a previously written short, engaging story. Read the story with enthusiasm. Ask volunteers to retell the beginning of the story, reminding children that the beginning usually introduces the characters, setting, and situation. Authors want to provide a strong beginning to "hook" the reader into wanting to continue. Next, ask volunteers to retell the middle of the story, reminding children that this is typically where details and events are explained and take place. Conclude by asking volunteers to retell the story ending. Explain that the ending often tells the reader how the situation was resolved. Further explain that just as the beginning of a story needs to "hook" the reader into wanting to continue, the ending should provide a satisfying conclusion for the reader.

2. Display several trade books that children have previously heard or read. Help them retell the stories, but read aloud the endings. Include books with a variety of endings.

3. Begin a class chart entitled, "Everyone Loves a Great Ending!" Brainstorm types of endings along with an example of each. Include:

   - fairytale endings
   - endings which surprise the reader
   - endings with an unanswered question
   - endings which answer a previously asked question
   - endings which restate the beginning of the story

4. Display a second short story which you previously prepared. Purposely do not include a satisfying ending. Read the story aloud. Lead children to conclude that the story does not have an ending.

5. Working in small groups, have children create an ending for your story. Each group should be prepared to share its ending with the class.

Revisiting the Lesson

As you read aloud to children, occasionally discuss the type of ending a story has.

You Will Need

- two stories previously written by you, one with no ending
- several familiar trade books with a variety of endings

Assessment Connection

While reviewing children's writing, note whether or not they are demonstrating an understanding of ending a story. Continue to model this skill with small groups of children as needed.

Writing About a Picture

You Will Need

- interesting, colorful pictures cut from magazines
- chart paper
- markers
- children's writing paper

Prepare for the mini-lesson by looking through old magazines and cutting out pictures that show action and detail—canoeing down a river, a soccer game, a birthday party scene, and so on. You should have more pictures than you do children in the class. Select one large picture and attach it to the top of a sheet of chart paper.

Assessment Connection

When children are stuck for story ideas, encourage them to check the idea box to see if looking at a picture helps. Discuss pictures with children as needed, helping them identify simple plots for their own stories.

Lesson Background

Young authors sometimes have trouble coming up with subjects for their writing. This mini-lesson helps to "jump start" children's imaginations by inviting them to write about interesting, action-packed pictures.

Teaching the Lesson

Introduce the lesson by discussing your thoughts about the image. I found this picture in a magazine and cut it out because it was so interesting. What do you think is going on? Yes, it does look like the two boys could be running a race. What else could be happening? Yes, they could be running away from something, or hurrying to get somewhere.

This picture helps me to think of all kinds of stories. Here's one. *Under the picture, record two or three sentences to accompany the action shown, reading aloud as you write. For example:*

> The boys raced across the field as fast as they could go. They had found a beehive high up in a tree. Now the bees were chasing them!

I like my story beginning. It tells about the picture. It also tells about some things I imagined—like finding the beehive and getting chased. And I can think of things to add to the story later. I want to explain how the boys get away from the bees!

Having a picture to look at is a good way to get ideas to write about. You can try it, too. You may choose one of the pictures I have here, or a picture you have drawn yourself. Take a few minutes to look at the picture. Think about what could be happening. Think about what might have happened before that—and what might happen afterward. If you want to, you can name the people or animals you see. Then write a short story to go with your picture. *As children work, add an ending to your own story. Then circulate, helping with ideas as needed. Display completed stories and the pictures that inspired them, or collate stories and pictures into a class anthology.*

Revisiting the Lesson

Create a file of story starters by placing cut-out pictures into an idea box in the classroom writing center. When children need help coming up with story ideas, have them consult the idea box and choose a picture to write about. Make old magazines available as well. Children can find other pictures to use for their own writing or to add to the box.

Writing a Long Story

Lesson Background

Young children do not always realize that they may continue their writing on to the next page when necessary. Instead, they sometimes believe that the story must stop at the end of the page. We can help children understand the idea of continuing writing from one page to another by providing explicit instruction and modeling.

You Will Need

an incomplete story written by you

Teaching the Lesson

1. Following a read-aloud, display the last page of the book and tell children to look at the page number. Lead them to observe that the story was not written on just one page, but continued for many pages.

2. Explain to children that they too may continue their stories from one page to another. Return to the book you have just read aloud. Browse through several pages, rereading if necessary, to confirm that although the reader has come to the end of a page, the story does continue. If possible, point to an example of a sentence continuing on the following page.

3. Display a story that you have previously started to write on chart paper. Read it aloud to children, explaining that you have not yet finished your story. In front of children, add a few more sentences to complete your work. Arrange this so that you will run out of space on the chart paper. Before continuing on to the next page, ask children what they think you should do. Following their responses, continue writing on the next page. After the story is complete, read it entirely as you run your hand under the text. When you get to the end of the first page, pause and remind yourself aloud that the story has not ended but instead is continued on the next page.

4. During independent writing time, you may wish to work with a smaller group of children whom you feel are ready to write long stories. Provide each child with two sheets of writing paper, stapled together in one corner. Put a small arrow at the bottom right-hand corner of the top page as a reminder to continue the story on the next page.

Revisiting the Lesson

Occasionally, after reading the first page of a new big book, act as though the story has ended. When children urge you to continue, explain that since you finished the first page, you assumed the story was done. Lead them to remind you that long stories continue from one page to another.

Writing Letters and Cards

You Will Need

- large teddy bear shape, with features
- five labels: Heading, Greeting, Body, Closing, Signature
- 8 1/2" x 11" copies of teddy bear shape, blank

Assessment Connection

As children complete letters and cards, note those who have trouble remembering the basic sections, their placement, and/or correct capitalization and punctuation. Children who need more help may benefit from having a model letter on display in the classroom or in their writing folders.

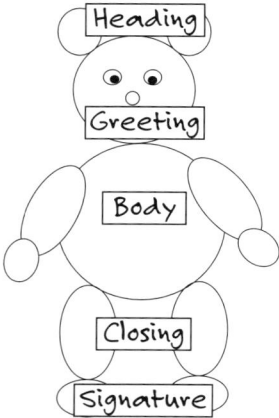

Lesson Background

In kindergarten, children are introduced to writing in the form of letters and cards. This mini-lesson offers a more formal introduction to the friendly letter and its parts.

Teaching the Lesson

1. Display the teddy bear, explaining that it is the class's "Friendly Letter Bear." The bear will help them learn and remember the parts of a friendly letter. Take them through the parts of a letter, using language such as "A letter starts with a heading that includes your address and the date." Place the "Heading" label at the top of the bear's head. "Then there is a greeting, which is like saying 'Hello.' It tells who you are writing to." Place the "Greeting" label near the bear's mouth. Continue through the rest of the friendly letter format, placing the "Body" label on the bear's body; the "Closing" label on the legs, and the "Signature" label on the feet.

2. Next have children help you compose a group letter to someone. The letter could be to thank a classroom visitor for coming, invite the principal to visit, show appreciation to lunchroom staff, or any other purpose that would be meaningful to children. Write the letter on chart paper, referring to the Friendly Letter Bear and reviewing the function, format, and punctuation of each section as it is written. When the letter is done, read it aloud to decide if anything needs to be changed. Explain that you will copy the letter so it can be delivered. (Or, if no changes need to be made, you can deliver the chart paper letter.)

3. Distribute copies of the teddy bear shape. Explain that children can add features to their own Friendly Letter Bears. Then they should label the bear with the parts of a friendly letter. They can keep the bear in their writing folders to remind them of the correct format of a letter.

Revisiting the Lesson

Choose an occasion for sending cards—individual thank-yous or invitations, cards for Father's Day, Mother's Day, a national holiday, and so on. Have children fold paper into fourths to make blank cards and decorate the fronts. Then walk them through the format for the inside of the card, stressing its similarity to the form of a friendly letter: heading (date), greeting, body, closing, and signature. Have children complete and deliver or mail their cards.

Writing a New Adventure for a Character

Lesson Background

Many authors write multiple books based on the same main characters. Children quickly become comfortable with the characters and want to read or hear more stories about their adventures. We can build on children's interest and enthusiasm by encouraging them to write new adventures for their favorite characters.

Teaching the Lesson

1. Read aloud one of the many *Franklin* books such as *Franklin and the Tooth Fairy, Franklin Goes to School,* or *Franklin Is Lost.* If not available, select another book from a series such as Norman Bridwell's *Clifford* books or Mercer Mayer's *Critter* stories.

2. Following the read-aloud, lead a discussion about Franklin's attributes. Record children's comments on chart paper by creating a web with Franklin's name in the center and the attributes surrounding it. Children may say, for example, that Franklin is kind, sometimes shy, a good problem solver, a good friend, and honest.

3. On chart paper, write a new adventure for Franklin. Perhaps Franklin might visit your school only to discover that the class wants to keep him as a pet! Encourage children to help you compose the story. When completed, read the story aloud. Referring back to the web, remind children that while the adventure is new, Franklin's attributes remained the same. In this new adventure, Franklin continues to be kind, sometimes shy, and so on.

4. During independent writing time, encourage children to create a new adventure for Franklin or another favorite character or have them incorporate the character into a story they are working on.

Revisiting the Lesson

With children, brainstorm a list of possible adventures, for example, climbing the highest mountain, moving to a new city, finding a treasure map, and getting lost on a family vacation. Write each adventure on a separate card. Place these "adventure cards" in the writing center or a central location. Encourage children to refer to the cards if they are in need of an idea for their writing. They can feature a favorite story character in their adventure if they wish. Add cards throughout the school year as children provide new suggestions.

Adding on to Familiar Poems and Songs

Lesson Background

Young children sometimes find it difficult to begin writing. Adding lines to a familiar poem or song is often less overwhelming than creating an entire story.

Teaching the Lesson

Before beginning the lesson, write the words to the first verse of the familiar rhyme "Mary Had a Little Lamb" on chart paper. On another sheet of paper, write the first couplet of "Humpty Dumpty." Keep the rhymes covered.

Let's say the rhyme "Mary Had a Little Lamb" together. *Then show children the words written on chart paper.* Can you tell me which words rhyme in this poem? That's right, *snow* and *go* rhyme. What other words rhyme with these words? *List the words children suggest.*

It's fun to write new verses for old rhymes. Here's one I thought of. *Write the following verse on the chart paper:*

Mary had a little cat
It's fur was soft as silk.
Mary fed her cat each day
With tuna fish and milk.

Does anyone have an idea for another verse about Mary? *Elicit responses from children and help them shape verses into new lines with two words that rhyme. Record their rhyme on the chart as well.*

Here's the beginning of a rhyme you all know. *Display the chart with the first couplet of "Humpty Dumpty" and read the rhyme in unison with children.* What words rhyme here? Yes, *wall* and *fall* rhyme.

Now you can write a new verse for "Humpty Dumpty." Think of two words that rhyme, like *dog* and *fog* or *road* and *toad.* Then change the words of the poem to write your new verse. You can change everything except the words *Humpty Dumpty.* Both lines of your new verse should start with Humpty's name. *Give children time to write their new rhymes. Then ask for volunteers to share their work. Record each new verse on the chart.*

Revisiting the Lesson

Provide a blank notebook and several familiar poems and songs in the writing center. Encourage children to add on to these songs and poems when visiting the center. If they wish, they may add their verses and illustrations to the notebook provided. Allow children to read their verses from the Author's Chair.

Retelling Favorite Stories and Poems

Lesson Background

Another good way to get children started on a story when they've run out of ideas is to suggest that they retell a favorite story or poem. By translating an existing work into their own words, they reinforce their sense of story, their knowledge of story elements, and their recall and summarizing skills. This is not a technique you would want children to turn to consistently, but it is a strategy with definite literacy value.

You Will Need

a book to read aloud

Teaching the Lesson

1. Following the read-aloud of an especially appealing book, engage children in a discussion about the story. Encourage them to share favorite parts, illustrations, surprises, and characters. Conclude the discussion by explaining that when you enjoy a favorite story or poem, it is fun to tell someone else about it.

2. Model a retelling of the story you just read. Write on chart paper as you think aloud. Begin with a graphic organizer such as a story map or flowchart, or simply write in paragraph format. When finished, read your work aloud with children.

3. Ask children whether or not your retelling would explain the story to someone who had not read it. Explain that when they retell a story, they should include enough details to make sense, tell the story in the same sequence as it was written, and try to avoid adding to the story.

4. After your retelling has been sufficiently modeled and discussed, give children an opportunity to recall favorite stories or poems. Then have children create their own written retellings, using graphic organizers if neccessary.

Revisiting the Lesson

Create three simple cards: retell the beginning, retell the middle, and retell the ending. After reading aloud to children, distribute the cards to three volunteers. Allow time for the volunteers to share their retelling. Remind children that a retelling is brief, not overly detailed, and sequential. Occasionally, record children's retellings on chart paper and display it for several days.

Assessment Connection

When conferencing with children about a story they have read, ask them to retell the story in a few sentences. Assess their ability to select important details to include.

Writing Nonfiction

Assessment Connection

You may wish to spend a few moments conducting a one-on-one assessment. Place before a child an array of books. Be certain to include a mix of fiction and nonfiction. Ask the child to sort the books according to whether they are fiction or nonfiction. Then ask the child to sort pieces from his or her writing folder according to whether they are fiction or nonfiction.

Teacher Tip

Be sure to include nonfiction in your read-aloud and shared-reading experiences. Children should also be familiar with the term *nonfiction* prior to conducting this mini-lesson.

Lesson Background

Some children become hooked on reading when they discover nonfiction. However, many children continue to think of writing as the process of making up stories. As teachers, we have the pleasure and obligation to introduce children to the joys of reading *and* writing nonfiction.

Teaching the Lesson

1. Display the fiction and nonfiction big books side by side. Read both titles and ask for some predictions about the books. What might each book be about? How might the books be alike? How might they be different? Help children conclude that one book looks like it tells a story and the other looks like it gives information.

2. Flip through the books to confirm children's predictions. You may want to read aloud a page or two of each book. Review or introduce the terms *fiction* and *nonfiction*.

3. Display an assortment of fiction and nonfiction books. Give children time to look through the books. Then have them sort the books into two piles—fiction and nonfiction. As children add books to the piles, ask them to explain how they made their decisions.

4. Next tell children that they are going to do some nonfiction writing themselves. Explain that authors of nonfiction have to know or learn facts about their topic. Help children realize that there are topics they already know a lot about. Suggest a topic related to something currently being studied by the class, such as dinosaurs, colors, or shapes.

5. Write the topic at the top of a sheet of chart paper. Then brainstorm with children a list of things they know about the topic. When the list is done, review it together. For each item on the list, ask, "Is this a fact or is it something we made up?"

6. Provide each child with a sheet of lined paper that has space for illustration. Ask them to consult the fact chart as they write two or three factual sentences about the topic. After children have finished their sentences, they may illustrate them. Then collect all the papers and staple them together in book form. Ask volunteers to make a cover and write a title for the book.

Revisiting the Lesson

During shared reading, take time to identify books as fiction or nonfiction. Discuss what makes each story either fiction or nonfiction.

Interviewing

Lesson Background

Young children are usually most comfortable writing about personal experiences. While we accept and celebrate this, we can also encourage children to write about a wider variety of topics. Teaching children to conduct simple interviews will allow them to gather information they can use when writing about an unknown topic.

You Will Need

one or more nonfiction books written by Gail Gibbons

Teaching the Lesson

1. Read aloud one of Gail Gibbons's nonfiction books such as *Milk Makers* or *Up Goes the Skyscraper.* If possible, display several more books by this author.

2. Following the read-aloud, ask children how author Gail Gibbons might have known so much about the book's topic. Lead children to conclude that the author had to learn about the topic before writing about it, and that one way to learn about something is to interview an expert or knowledgeable person.

3. Ask a volunteer to sit with you in front of the class. Explain that you are going to model an interview by asking the volunteer several questions about himself or herself. Conduct a brief interview, jotting down the child's responses. Explain that this information will help you later when you write about this person. Then, write a paragraph or two using the information you obtained during the interview. (Alternatively, you may wish to arrange to interview a staff member who has an unusual hobby or talent.)

4. During independent writing time, have children write three to five questions they will ask during an interview with someone in the class. Provide time for children to conduct the interviews. Encourage each child to write a paragraph about the person whom he or she interviewed.

Revisiting the Lesson

Encourage children to brainstorm a list of possible writing topics that may require a prewriting interview. For example, in writing about the day they were born, their parents could be interviewed. The school principal might be interviewed by someone who is writing about his or her school. To write about how to take care of pets, one might interview a veterinarian. Encourage children to develop questions they might ask in an interview with someone on the list.

Writing from Patterned Text

You Will Need

- sample "I Can" book (See Teaching the Lesson)
- copies of "I Can" book pages, one per child
- 2" x 11" strips of construction paper, two per child; two for sample book

Assessment Connection

Check children's patterned writing to see if they have mastered the concept of changing the words while sticking to the pattern. Invite more capable writers to develop their own ideas for patterns.

I can_____.
I can_____.
I can_____.
I can_____.
I can_____.

I can_____.

Lesson Background

A simple way to get even reluctant writers to write is to provide them with patterned text to use as story starters. Children can quickly produce writing they will be proud of by merely changing a few words in the pattern.

Teaching the Lesson

1. Prepare for the lesson by making a book master page. Draw horizontal lines every two inches down a sheet of 8 1/2" x 11" paper. (You will have five 2" strips and one 1" strip left at the bottom of the page.) Starting about an inch from the left of each 2" space, write the sentence starter, "I can." To make a sample book, cut the five strips apart, complete each sentence with something you can do, and staple the pages together on the left. Use two strips of construction paper to make a cover for the book.

2. Share your sample book by reading it aloud to children. After you finish reading, ask children what they notice about the words in the book. Help them conclude that each page starts with the same phrase. Explain that your book is a "pattern book." Only a few words change on each page.

3. Tell children that they can write their own "I Can" pattern books. Give each child one copy of the book strips and have them cut the five strips apart. Then have them add words to the "I can" sentence starter on each page to tell about things they can do. Children can illustrate their pages as well.

4. After children have finished their story sentences, ask them to put them in the order they want. Then let children choose construction paper strips for covers. Staple the covers and pages together at the left. After children decorate their covers and add the title "I Can," ask volunteers to share their books by reading them aloud.

Revisiting the Lesson

- Place blank strips of paper in the writing center. Post ideas for story starters and invite children to create new pattern books based on those ideas. Some suggestions for patterns are: I like..., I saw..., I am..., A friend (dog/cat/mother/father/grandparent) is..., and so on.

- Share a book that has a more advanced pattern, such as *Brown Bear, Brown Bear, What Do You See?* by Bill Martin, Jr., or *Ask Mr. Bear* by Marjorie Flack. Create a group book based on the same pattern.

Writing a How-to

Lesson Background

Children should learn that a "how-to" is a specific kind of writing. They need to realize that how-to directions must be written in clear language and in logical order. This mini-lesson will give them practice in putting directions in the correct order, which in turn will help them with both reading and writing this text structure.

Teaching the Lesson

Prior to the lesson, make a rock paperweight by following the directions at the right. Also cut apart the sets of directions and put individual sets into envelopes, one envelope per child. How many of you like to make things? So do I. It's fun to know how to make something—and to be able to tell someone else how to do it too. Here is something I made at home. *Show children your rock paperweight.* It's a paperweight I made from a smooth rock. I can use it on my desk to hold papers down.

Would you each like to make a paperweight of your own? I thought you might, so I wrote the instructions down for you. This kind of writing is called a "how-to." Today we are going to read the directions together. I put a copy in an envelope for each of you. *Distribute the envelopes and have children open them.* Oh, I see a problem. The directions are out of order. Do you think that matters? *Help children conclude that when making something, the order of steps in the process can make a difference. For example, they shouldn't put their smocks on after painting.*

Read each of the directions to yourself. Think about what order makes sense and arrange the strips on your desk in that order. I will check your directions and give you another sheet of paper so you can glue them down in order. Then later you can use your how-to directions to make your own paperweight. *Circulate around the room, checking children's directions. You can accept the directions in an order different than shown at the right, as long as the steps still make sense.*

Revisiting the Lesson

- Later, give children a chance to read and follow the directions. This will enable them to see how ordering the sentences helps the reader. Be sure to supply the necessary materials: art smocks, acrylic paint, brushes, fine-line markers—and rocks.

- Invite children to make their own "how-to" directions to show others how to make or do something. You may want to post these how-to's in a center and actually let children try them.

Assessment Connection

Note children who seem to have trouble following or writing directions. Before doing or writing a how-to, have the child go through the steps in the process with you orally.

Reading Your Work to Yourself

You Will Need

- a piece of your writing recorded on chart paper
- a marker

Lesson Background

When young children finish a piece of writing, they often want to either share it right away or put it away, as if it is a completed work. We must help children understand the importance of rereading their work to themselves so that they can make sure their writing is the best it can be.

Teaching the Lesson

1. Explain to the class that you will read a short story to them. Tell children that they are to be quiet observers, listening to you as though you were reading your story to yourself. Tell them that the reason you are rereading your story is to make sure you have written everything that you wanted to before you share it with a friend. Read the story you have written on chart paper to the class.

2. As you read, think aloud about words, phrases, or details that you may have forgotten to add to your story. Be sure to add one or two "forgotten" details to your story.

3. Read your story aloud one more time before announcing that you are "done." Explain to the class that writers ask themselves questions such as "Am I really done?" "Do I like my story?" "What else could I write about in this story?" "Will my friends understand my story?" "What will they want to know about as I read my story to them?" (List the questions on the chalkboard as you ask them.)

4. Ask children to each select one story in progress from their writing portfolios. Explain to children that once they have reread their story and asked themselves these questions, they may find a friend to share the story with.

Revisiting the Lesson

- During writing time, ask a volunteer to let you share an example of his or her writing with the class. Talk through the writing as you did with your own.

- As a class, brainstorm a list of questions writers might ask themselves when they finish a piece of writing. Write the list on chart paper to post in the room for children's reference.

Reading to a Peer or Group

Lesson Background

Children are encouraged to read their written work to a peer or a group for several important reasons. Reading aloud:

- is the beginning step in conferencing with a peer or teacher.

- enables the writer to hear and see another person's response and reaction.

- provides practice in acquiring public speaking skills.

- affords the writer another opportunity to determine whether or not further revision is needed.

Teaching the Lesson

1. Reading aloud to children on a daily basis provides constant modeling of appropriate read-aloud behavior. After a read-aloud, tell children that they will soon be encouraged to read their writing aloud to a peer or group. Invite children to help you create guidelines for reading aloud. Write these guidelines on chart paper to display in the classroom. You may wish to include the following:

   - Take a deep breath before beginning and smile at your audience.

   - Use a clear voice.

   - Read with lots of expression.

   - Have fun reading out loud.

2. Have each child find a partner, or assign a partner to each child. Instruct them to take turns reading aloud a piece of their own writing. After children have had ample time to read aloud to their peers, come together as a whole group. Discuss what was hard about reading aloud. What guidelines were helpful? Add to your list of guidelines if necessary.

Revisiting the Lesson

Refer to the read-aloud guidelines as needed. Occasionally, you may wish to have a pair of volunteers model peer conferencing, including reading their work aloud, to the entire class.

You Will Need

- a read-aloud book
- chart paper
- marker
- children's own writing

Assessment Connection

Some children may have difficulty reading aloud to a peer or group. Being nervous and/or immature may lead some to act silly or withdrawn. Periodically, record your observations of individual children reading aloud. Be sure to take time to review previous observations so that you may determine whether or not progress is being made.

Listening and Asking Questions

You Will Need

- chart paper
- marker

Assessment Connection

Record your informal observations of each child's listening and questioning behaviors. Periodically review your observations to help determine if any children are displaying consistently unusual listening or questioning behaviors. For example, a child who often asks questions which do not relate to the topic at hand may be experiencing auditory processing difficulties.

Lesson Background

Participating in an editing conference requires each person to listen and to ask appropriate questions. Young children may improve their listening and questioning behaviors as we provide explicit instruction and modeling of these important communication skills.

Teaching the Lesson

1. Explain to children that an editing conference is most successful when each person involved uses good listening and questioning behaviors. As a group, brainstorm and record on chart paper statements that complete the sentence: "A good listener...." For example, "A good listener is quiet and waits for the speaker to finish before talking."

2. Lead a discussion about asking questions. Allow children to brainstorm what may be appropriate and what may not be. For example, when your friend is reading aloud, it is not appropriate to ask if he or she packed a lunch or is buying lunch today. Conclude that only questions about the writing should be asked, and they should be asked to be helpful to the writer, not to criticize.

3. Ask a volunteer to read his or her writing aloud to you as you model good listening and questioning. You may wish to model this a second time, demonstrating what poor listening and inappropriate questions look and sound like.

4. Have children choose partners and role-play listening and asking questions. Explain that one child should read aloud a paragraph from a favorite story. The listener must ask one good question about what he or she heard. Children can switch roles. As children role-play, circulate and offer guidance where necessary.

Revisiting the Lesson

Occasionally, just after reading aloud, share with children specific good listening and questioning behaviors you noticed. For example, "Kyle, I noticed that you sat still and looked at me as I read. Sarah, you asked a really good question about the ladder that suddenly became available just when the dog needed it."

Asking for Comments

Lesson Background

As part of the writing process, children can gain valuable feedback by asking a listener for comments. Young children, however, may not inherently know how to ask questions that are specific enough to be helpful. We can model the types of questions to ask and how to use the feedback to edit writing.

Teaching the Lesson

1. Read aloud a story that you have previously written. When finished, ask several specific questions about your story. For example, "Did the beginning of my story interest you so that you wanted to hear the rest, or was it uninteresting? Was any part of my story confusing to you? Did you wish there were more or fewer details? Did you find my story funny (or sad, or mysterious, etc.)? Did the ending satisfy you or do you still wonder about something?"

2. Using children's feedback, make one or two changes to your story. Then reread your story to the class. Explain that asking for children's comments helped you decide whether or not you wanted to make changes to your story. Explain that during a writing conference with either a peer or you, they too should ask the listener for his or her comments. Remind them that you asked very specific questions so that the comments would be helpful. Had you simply asked, "Did you like my story?" you probably would have heard the comment, "Yes." This would not be a helpful comment.

3. During independent writing time, encourage children to read their work to a peer. Remind children to ask the listener for his or her comments just as you did after reading your story aloud.

Revisiting the Lesson

With children, brainstorm a list of possible questions a writer might ask after reading his or her work aloud. You may wish to display the list or provide each child with a copy to keep in his or her writing folder. As children become more experienced in peer conferencing, you might ask two volunteers to model a conference for the class.

You Will Need

- a brief story previously written by you

Assessment Connection

As you occasionally observe peer conferences, note whether or not the reader asks the listener for comments. If not, you may wish to join in the conference and model how to ask for comments. Also, note whether the writer considers using the listener's comments when editing his or her work.

Conferencing with the Teacher

Lesson Background

Conferencing with individuals provides a wonderful opportunity to meet the specific needs of each child. Conferencing is equally beneficial for the child, who is given the teacher's undivided attention, encouragement, and guidance.

Teaching the Lesson

1. Explain to children that during independent writing time, you will meet with individual children to discuss their writing progress. Enthusiastically tell children that this is a great opportunity for you to get to know how they are doing with their writing. Further explain that this meeting is referred to as a conference.

2. Briefly tell children what they may expect when conferencing with you. This may include procedures such as where the conference will take place, how to request a conference, how children will know when it is their turn to meet with you, and what they should bring to the conference. Reaffirm that the purpose of conferencing is to meet each child's specific needs, so each conference may be a little different.

3. Ask a volunteer to help you model a writing conference for the class. Be sure that the rest of the children can see and hear as you conduct this brief conference.

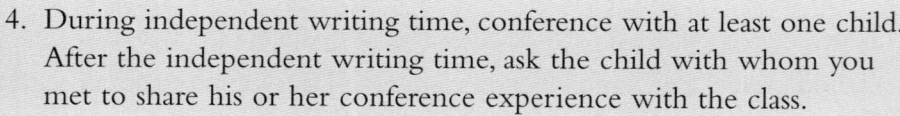
4. During independent writing time, conference with at least one child. After the independent writing time, ask the child with whom you met to share his or her conference experience with the class.

Revisiting the Lesson

You may wish to create a conferencing checklist for display in the classroom or to be placed in each child's writing folder. The checklist might include these questions: Do I have something to share with my teacher? Do I have one or two questions to ask? Have I practiced reading my work aloud? Have I made any changes to my work because of my last conference? Is my writing folder organized? Remind children to refer to the checklist before conferencing with you.

Conferencing with Peers

Lesson Background

A classroom is a community of learners. Peer conferencing promotes such an environment by encouraging children to assist one another with the writing process.

Teaching the Lesson

1. Explain to children that a peer conference is an opportunity to share their own writing with a classmate who will give them feedback and suggestions. Tell children that you will model for them what might happen during a peer conferencing session.

2. Select a child who has finished writing a first draft. Ask the child to help you model peer conferencing for the class. Sit beside the child with his or her writing in front of you. Be sure that the rest of the children are able to see and hear you. Ask the child to read his or her work aloud to you. When finished, compliment the child. Proceed to ask the child a question or two if the story needs any clarification. Make one or two simple suggestions. Say, for example, "I really enjoyed how you described your baby sister! Maybe you could add a sentence about how she acts now that she is older." Briefly help the child brainstorm a sentence to add. Allow time for it to be written down. Ask the child if he or she has any questions for you. Finally, look at the writing and bring any errors (spelling, punctuation, spacing, etc.) to the writer's attention.

3. After modeling this for children, point out to them that peer conferencing is not limited to reading aloud to a friend. Rather, this is an opportunity for the writer to gain valuable feedback to assist in final editing.

4. While children are involved in a writing project or assignment, look for children who may be ready to conference with a peer. Until children are comfortable with the procedure, you may wish to sit in on a few conferences.

Revisiting the Lesson

Together with children, create a list of peer conferencing guidelines on chart paper. Determine at what point a writer is ready to engage in a peer conference, where and for how long the conference should take place, how children may select a peer for the conference, and how a conference should proceed.

Assessment Connection

Occasionally, sit behind two children as they conference. Explain that you are going to be a quiet observer. Maintaining anecdotal notes about these sessions is an excellent way to track progress over time.

What's Important, What's Not

You Will Need

- a story prepared by you that includes several unimportant details
- a card for each child on which *important* is written on one side and *unimportant* on the other side

Lesson Background

Young children's writing often leans toward one of two extremes: far too many details or far too few. We must help children understand that they should edit their writing to find a balance between the two extremes.

Teaching the Lesson

1. Explain to children that all good writers edit their work to check things like spelling, sentence flow, and proper sequencing. Writers must also be certain that the information they have included is necessary and important to the story or text. Too many unimportant details confuse and bore the reader.

2. Explain that children are going to help you edit your story to determine what is important and what is not. Further explain that unimportant details will be crossed out or "cut." Read your story aloud without interruption. Next, provide each child with a card on which the word *important* is written on one side and the word *unimportant* is written on the other side. Read the story again, pausing after each sentence to allow children time to decide which side of the card each wishes to display. As a group, discuss and agree on which sentences to cut from your story. Model drawing lines through sentences, phrases, or words to show that they are to be cut from the final copy. You may wish to repeat this lesson using a child's writing. (Be sure to have the child's permission before doing so.)

3. During independent writing time, encourage children to read their work to a peer. The peer may use the important/unimportant card to help the writer determine whether or not any sentences need to be cut.

Revisiting the Lesson

When reading aloud to children, occasionally omit an important detail. Pause at the end of the page or paragraph, asking children whether or not the story is making sense. After rereading the page correctly, lead children to conclude that the missing sentence was a necessary and important detail for the reader.

Adding Details

Lesson Background

Young children often have little difficulty orally sharing the details of a story or personal experience. Committing these stories to paper, however, may be an overwhelming task for beginning writers. The result is typically a few short, nondescript sentences. With instruction and modeling, we can help children recognize the value of adding meaningful details to their writing.

Teaching the Lesson

1. Before class, write a short, nondescriptive story. For example: "I had a dog. His name was Freedom. He ran away. But then we got him back." Read the story aloud to children. Ask them if they have questions for you, the author, or if the story provided enough details. Encourage children to ask questions such as "What kind of dog was Freedom? How old were you when this happened? Why did he run away? How did you get him back?"

2. Rewrite the story, adding the information children requested. Reread the completed story, concluding that the revised text is more enjoyable for the reader. Explain that when a writer adds details, he or she is helping the reader better understand and visualize the story events. A good story includes details that help make it more interesting and satisfying for the reader.

3. Have each child write two or three sentences about seeing a real or imaginary animal. Then have them choose partners. They can take turns reading the sentences aloud, asking questions, and adding at least one detail to their writing.

Revisiting the Lesson

- With their permission, children's writing samples may be used to repeat this lesson as needed.

- Model for children how to read a rough draft to a peer. After listening, the peer should ask any unanswered questions. The writer uses this feedback when writing a final draft by adding some of the details suggested.

You Will Need

a story written previously by you

Teacher Tip

You may wish to tape-record a child telling a story. Assist the child in putting into writing the most important parts of the story. Then have him or her add details. This process, storytelling into story writing, may also be modeled for the whole group.

Proofreading Symbols: Caret, Delete Line

You Will Need

Write the following on a piece of chart paper or on the chalkboard:

Twinkle, twinkle, little blue star,
How wonder where you might be.
Up above the great big world so high,
Like a ruby in the sky.

Lesson Background

When writers want to make corrections to their writing, they use proofreading symbols to show what and where these corrections should be. Young children can learn to use two basic marks, a caret and a delete line, to help them revise their writing.

Teaching the Lesson

1. Explain to children that when writers reread their work, they often make changes or corrections to what they've written. There are special marks that writers use to show what these changes are. Sometimes they need to add words, sometimes they need to get rid of words, and sometimes they just want to change their wording.

2. Write a caret mark on the board, and tell children that this mark is used to add something to a sentence. Then write a delete line on the board and tell children that this mark is used to take something away in a sentence.

3. Show children only the first line of the poem (cover the other three lines with a piece of paper) and read it out loud. Ask children if the line is written the way they remember it. Ask what is wrong. Have the first child who suggests *blue* does not belong come up and draw a delete line through the word. (You may want to demonstrate the correct placement of the symbols the first time.)

4. Now uncover the second line and read it out loud. First ask if children think there is something missing. The first child who identifies the missing word *I* should come up and draw a caret mark and write the word *I* above it. Then ask if anything else is wrong with the line. Have volunteers come up and use correct marks to fix the rest of the line.

5. Ask children to copy the last two lines of the poem onto a piece of paper. Ask them to work with a partner and, using a caret mark and a delete line, correct the lines.

Revisiting the Lesson

Use a short piece of writing, either something of your own or something from a favorite book, to demonstrate altering the writing by using a caret mark and a delete line. You might choose to change the character's name, the focus of the piece, or the outcome. Ask children to reread a piece of writing they are currently working on and make corrections using these two proofreading symbols.

Proofreading Symbols: Upper- and Lowercase Letters, Punctuation

Lesson Background

This mini-lesson will add to children's proofreading vocabulary—and give them more symbols to use when marking changes to their writing. Use this lesson after the mini-lesson, *Caret and Delete Line*.

Teaching the Lesson

Write the following sentence on the chalkboard: The boys boys ran down street. You have already learned how to use the caret and delete line when marking changes in your writing. Can anyone show me how we might use those proofreading symbols to mark this sentence? *Allow volunteers to use a delete line and caret to indicate the deletion of one* boys *and the addition of* the *before the word* street.

Today we are going to learn more proofreading symbols. Look at this story. *Display the paragraph below, written double-spaced on chart paper.*

> Tom has a dog named spot. Spot is a big dog. He has black Spots all over his back Do you think that is how he got his name

Does anyone see anything that needs to be changed in this story? Yes, the dog's name should start with a capital letter. This is how you show that a letter should be a capital when you proofread. *Use one color marker to draw three lines under letters that need to be capitalized, a different color to draw a slash through letters that need to be lowercase, and a third color to draw carets with correct punctuation where needed.*

On the chalkboard, write the three proofreading symbols, with explanations, as shown below:

≡　　　　　/　　　　　$\hat{?}$

capital letter　　lowercase letter　　missing punctuation mark

Now look at some writing that you have done. Check for letters that should be changed to a capital or lowercase letter. Check for missing periods, question marks, or commas. See if there are words you need to add or delete. Then use proofreading symbols to mark any changes you want to make to your writing.

Revisiting the Lesson

On individual sheets of paper, write different paragraphs that contain several errors. Laminate the pages and place them in an independent work center with erasable markers. Let children proofread the paragraphs, using proofreading symbols.

You Will Need

- sample text to proofread (See Teaching the Lesson), double-spaced on chart paper
- markers in three different colors

Assessment Connection

Note whether or not children begin to use proofreading symbols when checking their own work. Be sure you model the use of the symbols when you check their writing as well.

Checking Capitalization and Punctuation

You Will Need

On a piece of chart paper, write the following:

Capitalization
Have I capitalized the word *I* when it means me?
Have I capitalized people's names?
Have I capitalized the names of towns, cities, and countries?
Have I capitalized the first word in each sentence?

Punctuation
Do my questions end with a question mark?
If I'm making a statement, does the sentence end with a period?
If I'm excited about something, does that sentence end with an exclamation mark?
Do I have quotation marks around the exact words people are saying?
Are my commas in the right places?

Lesson Background

As part of the publishing process, writers check their work after they've written it to see if any changes are needed. Children as writers need to check that they've capitalized everything that needs capitalization and that the punctuation they've used is correct.

Teaching the Lesson

1. Explain to children that you are going to practice checking for capitalization and punctuation by writing a brief report on today's events, or "Daily News." Ask a volunteer to help you by explaining in one sentence something that happened at school that day. Explain that the volunteer should include any capitalization and punctuation necessary in the sentence. Write only what the volunteer tells you to write, regardless of whether the child remembers the capitalization and punctuation or not. At this point, do not comment if the child has omitted anything.

2. When the dictation is complete, read the sentence you've written to the class. With the class, review the checklist you made on chart paper, item by item, checking for capitalization and punctuation. If children find a mistake, ask a volunteer to come up and write the correction. If time permits, you may want to evaluate another sentence or two with the class, beginning with another volunteer who can suggest a sentence.

3. Tape the checklist on the wall for future reference.

4. Ask children to take out their writing folders or journals. Children should choose one sentence from one piece of writing to check for punctuation and capitalization. Read aloud each item on the checklist and give children time to read through their writing and make any necessary corrections.

Revisiting the Lesson

Keep the Capitalization and Punctuation chart on display in the classroom. Occasionally refer to the chart after you have posted written directions for a project. Have children help you check your directions, using the chart as a reference. You may want to purposely include an error so children can "correct" it for you.

Checking Spelling

Lesson Background

While we can't expect young writers to spell every word correctly, we can remind them of this aspect of revising and provide them with helpful tips on how to check their work for spelling errors.

Teaching the Lesson

1. As you are engaged in modeled writing (writing in front of the children while thinking aloud), tell them that you want to use a particular word but are unsure of its correct spelling. Ask children what they think you should do. Conclude that you will attempt to write the word but will circle it. This way, your thinking will not be interrupted, but you will be reminded to come back to the circled word to check it later. Suggest that children follow this procedure as they write.

2. After you have completed the modeled writing piece, return to the circled word. Together with children, brainstorm several ways to find the correct spelling of a word. For example, children may look for a word on the word wall or in other environmental print, in a dictionary or on personal word lists, or ask a friend for help.

3. Ask children to copy the following sentence, exactly as written:

   I like books about sience and soshul studies.

   Have them work independently to circle words that they think need to be checked for correct spelling. Then have them choose a partner and "search" for the correct spelling.

Revisiting the Lesson

- With the writer's permission, display a child's first draft so that all children can easily read it. Together, look at the words the writer has circled and determine how the correct spelling of each word may be found. Locate the correct spelling and write it above the circled word. Additionally, look for words that are spelled incorrectly but are not circled. Remind children that they must look carefully at their work for spelling errors.

- As a class, create a list of strategies for correcting a misspelled word. Your list might include: use a dictionary, use the word wall, ask a friend, and so on. Post the list in the room, adding to it or referring to it as necessary.

Assessment Connection

You may wish to use a child's first draft to assess whether or not obviously misspelled words have been circled. Further, monitor the child's ability to correct spelling errors so that the incorrect spelling is not copied onto the final copy.

Checking Sequence

You Will Need

- a story previously written by you
- red, yellow, and green markers
- paper that has been divided into three sections labeled *beginning, middle, ending* (at least one for each child)

Lesson Background

Because sequencing is a difficult skill for some children to master, we must provide them with ways in which to check their stories for correct sequencing.

Teaching the Lesson

1. Display a story that you previously prepared. Explain that your story is finished, but you want to check it to be sure that the beginning, middle, and ending are in the correct order, or sequence.

2. Read your story aloud without interruption. While reading it a second time, underline the beginning of the story with a green marker, the middle with a yellow marker, and the end with a red marker. Think aloud as you do this so that children may hear your thought process. For example, as you are reading aloud, you might say, "This is the beginning of my story. I know this because it 'hooks' the reader into wanting to continue reading. It also introduces the characters, setting, and/or problem. I will underline the beginning with a green marker because green reminds me of getting started. Now this is the part where I have written details and events. This is the middle of my story. I'll underline this using a yellow marker. I know that this is the ending because it tells the reader how the problem was resolved [or it surprises the reader, etc. I'll underline the ending with a red marker because red reminds me of stopping. Now, let me look back over my story. If the story is sequenced properly, I should see green marker used first, yellow second, and red last."

3. Encourage children to check the sequence of their own work using the method you modeled. Allow children who may not currently have a completed story to work with a peer who does have one. Alternatively, you may wish to provide small groups or pairs with a copy of a simple story that you prepared.

Assessment Connection

You may wish to use the children's beginning/middle/ending papers (from Revisiting the Lesson) or their completed stories with colored marker underlines as assessment pieces.

Revisiting the Lesson

Provide each child with a paper that has been divided into three sections. Each section should be labeled as follows: the first section "beginning," the second section "middle," and the third section "ending." Model how to write a first draft on this paper by writing in the appropriate sections. As you model this, begin by jotting down just a few ideas in each section and then go back and develop the ideas into more detailed text.

Checking Word Order

Lesson Background

In an effort to get thoughts onto paper before ideas are lost, writers sometimes inadvertently record words in an order that does not make sense to the reader. Young children may not check their work for proper word order unless we provide instruction and modeling to help them do so.

Teaching the Lesson

1. Explain that sometimes, without realizing it, we write words in an order that doesn't makes sense. Display the piece of writing that you prepared earlier. Read it without interruption, stumbling when you read the sentences with incorrect word order. When finished, ask children if your story made sense at all times. Help them to conclude that it does require some revision. As a class, edit all word order errors.

2. Share with children that reading your story aloud helped you hear word order errors. Suggest that they too read their work aloud to themselves, a peer, or a small group to help them check for proper word order.

3. Show children a tape recorder with a blank audiocassette. Explain that this is a tool to help check for word order errors. Read your short story aloud again, this time recording your reading. Play back the recording, pointing out that while listening to the story you keep the written copy in front of you. Model for children how to pause the tape player, look at the written copy, and make quick editing marks.

4. Demonstrate how to use the tape recorder, including the volume control. Explain that children will be rewinding the tape and recording over someone else's read-aloud. Place the tape recorder in a quiet corner of the classroom. Put up a sign-up sheet and encourage children to record themselves reading a piece of writing, then rewinding, listening, and editing the piece.

Revisiting the Lesson

Have children decide how they'd like to review their next piece of writing for correct word order. Have children discuss how the method they chose helped them.

You Will Need

- a short story of yours that includes a few word order errors
- a tape recorder and blank cassette

Teacher Tip

You may wish to create a center for this editing technique. Involve children in creating a name (Recording Studio, for example), a sign, and guidelines for the center.

Assessment Connection

Periodically, sit with children as they use the tape recorder. This will help you determine whether further modeling and instruction may be required.

Matching Words and Pictures

You Will Need

- a favorite big book that has lots of pictures and text that supports those pictures
- a big book that is unfamiliar to children

Assessment Connection

When conferencing about a child's writing, note whether or not illustrations match the text. If not, ask questions to determine why the child chose the illustration.

Lesson Background

At the beginning stages of writing, children draw pictures and write text to help tell their story. But the pictures and text don't always match. For instance, a child might draw a picture of a dog, while the text describes a trip to the grocery store. Children will be less likely to make these mistakes if they are made aware of good text/illustration matches.

Teaching the Lesson

1. Choose a big book that is one of children's favorites. With the class, read through the book, pointing out how the words and the pictures support each other. The text tells what is going on in the picture, and the picture gives the reader an idea of what is happening in the text. For each page ask, "Do the words tell about the picture? Does the picture tell about the words?"

2. Draw a simple picture on a piece of chart paper, such as a bear going fishing. Write a sentence below the picture that does not correlate, such as, "The bear likes to eat honey."

3. Allow time for children to respond. Point out that even though it's true that a bear likes to eat honey, that is not what the picture is about. Ask children what they could do to correct this problem. Suggest that they could either change the text or change the picture. Make the change that children suggest. Caution children that when they make a decision like this in their own stories, they should think about the kind of story they are writing and what it is about.

4. Display a page from the big book that is unfamiliar to children. Ask children to each write two sentences—one that goes with the picture and one that doesn't. When all children have written their sentences, have them trade papers with a partner. Children should then circle the sentence their partner wrote that does go with the picture. If time permits, have several volunteers read aloud their circled sentences.

Revisiting the Lesson

Divide the class into small groups and ask children to share a piece of their own writing that has pictures on it. The rest of the group will help the author decide if the pictures and the text match each other. Take turns until each child has shared a piece of writing and received feedback about his or her text/picture matching.

To Publish or Not to Publish

Lesson Background

After children publish their first pieces of writing, they often want the thrill of publishing everything they write. This lesson will help children understand what is appropriate for publishing. It will also allow reluctant children to continue writing without pressure to publish or share their work with others.

Teaching the Lesson

1. Tell children that you have finished two pieces of writing. Read both samples to children. Then explain that you are trying to decide what to do with your writing. Discuss the options available, such as putting your work in a writing folder, taking it home to share with your family, or publishing it in book format.

2. Explain that every author needs to think about whether or not to publish writing he or she has done. To help with that decision, authors can ask themselves questions about their work. Model and answer these questions aloud in relation to each of your samples: "Am I done with this story, or might I add more to it later? Would my friends be interested in reading this story? Did I write it for someone special? Do I want to share it with other people?"

3. Use your answers to the questions above to help you choose one piece to publish. Explain that later you will be talking about how to publish the work. Set the writing aside to use with the mini-lesson *Publishing.*

4. Ask children to look through their own writing folders to decide whether or not they are ready to publish something. Encourage them to ask themselves questions about their work, just as you did about yours. Have them mark a piece they want to publish.

Revisiting the Lesson

Share the following information about Laura Ingalls Wilder. Her daughter, Rose, thought her mother's stories of pioneer days would be interesting for others to read. So Laura decided to write her stories down. Her first manuscript, *Pioneer Girl,* has never been published. Editors rejected it. However, she rewrote and published part of it as a picture book, *When Grandma Was a Little Girl.* She then expanded it to become *Little House in the Big Woods.* This example will help illustrate for children how a story that may not be ready to be published can be changed and published later.

You Will Need

two short writing samples, written by you

Assessment Connection

Meet with children to talk about work they have decided to publish. Discuss with them some of the questions modeled in the mini-lesson to determine how they made their decisions.

Publishing

You Will Need

- several trade books, both fiction and nonfiction
- a child's final draft, ready for publication
- a child's illustrated cover for the finished book
- a center set up with publishing supplies

Teacher Tip

When you create your classroom publishing system, be sure to account for the following:

- Who will put the child's story into book format? You? The child? A volunteer?
- Who will decide when a piece is ready to publish or if it should be published? You? The child? Both of you together?
- What formats can published pieces take? Computer generated? Handwritten? Copied by an adult?
- Where will publishing supplies be kept? In a closet or center? On a shelf?
- What supplies will be available for final pages, covers, and binding?
- What steps in the process can children do independently? What steps will require assistance?

Lesson Background

As children develop as writers, it is important to have a publishing system available to them. By publishing children's stories, we validate their efforts and celebrate their successes. An established class system makes this process enjoyable for everyone.

Teaching the Lesson

1. Before teaching this lesson, you will need to have a classroom publishing system in place. Be sure to have the process set up in a clear, understandable way.

2. Once you have your plan established, introduce it to children. Begin by examining several trade books. Ask children to read the information on the covers. Talk about how the books are bound.

3. Explain that the author of each trade book wanted his or her book published so the story or information could be shared with readers. Go on to tell children that they are all authors too. They can share their work by publishing it themselves, in the classroom. They will be listed on the cover as the author of their own books.

4. Go through the publishing process, using a child's final draft as an example. Review how a draft gets to the final stage and how the decision is made to publish. Explain the various formats publishing can take and the options for binding. Then demonstrate how to put a book together. Be sure children understand where materials are located and how to use them.

Revisiting the Lesson

Review the publishing process as children use it to create books. Adapt elements of the process as needed to accommodate your unique learners.

Choosing a Title

Lesson Background

Young children often create titles based on simple label formats. If a child's story is about a dog, he may choose a title such as "My Dog." By calling attention to titles, you can model for children how to pick titles that will interest the reader.

Teaching the Lesson

1. Share several of the trade book titles you gathered with children. Talk about why each title gets your attention and why the author may have chosen that title. Discuss with children the importance of choosing a title that will grab the reader's attention. Then read your short story to the class. Tell them that authors often write their stories first and then choose a title. Tell them that authors may make a list of titles to choose from. Begin writing some title ideas on chart paper.

2. As you write your titles, include a few that have nothing to do with your story. Ask children to be thinking in their own minds which title they would choose for your story and why.

3. Upon completion of your title list, talk about each title and decide as a class if it would be a good title for your story. Why or why not? Have children help you decide the top three possibilities. Tell them that as the author you have the right to pick the final title, but that you will have to think carefully before deciding. Share your final title choice with them the following day.

4. When children finish a story, remind them to make a list of at least three titles that might go with their story. Encourage them to talk to a friend about the titles and then choose one.

Revisiting the Lesson

- Ask for several volunteers to share stories they have written with the class. Together, help the author list several possible titles. Remind children that the author has the final decision about the title.

- Select a variety of trade books that would be unfamiliar to children. Cover up the title on the front covers. Read one or more of the books to the class. Have children think of a title for the story, then see what the author chose by uncovering the title on the book cover. Discuss which title(s) children preferred—their suggestions or the author's choices.

You Will Need

- several trade books with interesting and appropriate titles
- chart paper
- markers

Write a short story to share with children. Do not give your story a title.

Assessment Connection

When conferencing with children, ask them why they selected the titles they did. Reinforce interesting and apt title choices.

Writing a Dedication

You Will Need

- selection of picture books with dedications (See Literature Connection)
- children's writing ready to be published
- 3" x 5" index cards

Teacher Tip

The following books offer a variety of dedication formats:

- *Little Polar Bear Finds a Friend* by Hans de Beer
- *Brother Eagle, Sister Sky* by Susan Jeffers
- *Dinotopia* by James Gurney
- *Carl's Christmas* by Alexandra Day
- *The Legend of Sleepy Hollow* retold by Robert San Souci
- *Something BIG Has Been Here* by Jack Prelutsky

Assessment Connection

When conferencing with children about their writing, look for dedications in work they consider ready for publication. Ask children to explain their dedications to you. If some children never spontaneously include a dedication in published work, encourage them to begin doing so.

Lesson Background

This mini-lesson makes children aware of the purpose of a dedication page and where it is located in a book. Children will also write meaningful dedications for their own writing.

Teaching the Lesson

1. Display a selection of picture books with dedications. Choose a book with a simple dedication, such as *Little Polar Bear Finds a Friend*. Discuss with children the elements of the cover—the title, author, illustration, and so on. Then go on to identify inside features such as the copyright page and title page. Point out the text of the dedication and read it aloud. Then introduce the term and ask children to think about why, and to whom, an author might dedicate a book.

2. Share a more detailed dedication, such as the one found in *Brother Eagle, Sister Sky*. Ask children to speculate about what this dedication might mean and why the author might have written it.

3. Invite children to look through the other books on display to locate and read the dedications. Then ask them to choose a piece of their own writing that is ready, or almost ready, for publication. Have them think about someone they want to honor with a dedication—and why. For example, a book could be dedicated to a friend or family member, someone who gave the writer an idea for a story, people who helped with the writing, or even a pet who inspired a story.

4. Offer children 3" x 5" index cards on which to record their dedications. Have them each share their dedications with a classmate and explain why and to whom they were written. Then, when writing is published, have children copy their dedications onto a special dedication page.

Revisiting the Lesson

Invite children to locate other interesting dedications in trade books. Photocopy these pages and dedication pages from children's own published work. Trim the photocopies to create interesting shapes and arrange in collage form on chart paper or a bulletin board. Title the collage "This Book is Dedicated to..." When you have a minute or two between activities, read aloud a dedication and invite children to speculate about why the author might have written it. Encourage children to refer to the collage for ideas when they want to write dedications in the future.

Finishing Illustrations and Labels

Lesson Background

When children begin to write, they often draw illustrations first and then add the words. Once they've added the words, they put the writing away and consider their work done. Instead, children should go back to their illustrations and make sure that they have completed their artwork and shown everything they intended to show when they wrote the text.

Teaching the Lesson

1. Show the pictures you drew of the two dogs. Ask children which one is a better picture and why, eliciting that the second picture provides the reader with more details about the dog. Point out that just as we include details in our writing to better communicate a story or an idea, we use details in our pictures to do the same thing.

2. Ask children to take out an illustrated writing sample and look at the picture again. Say, "Sometimes after we put away our work and bring it out later, we think of things we would like to include that we left out the first time. Are there any details that you would like to add to your picture now that may help a reader understand your story a little better?" Allow time for children to add to their drawings.

Revisiting the Lesson

- After a shared reading, review some of the story illustrations with children. Discuss whether or not the illustrator included all the important story details in his or her artwork. Encourage children to suggest details they think could be added.

- Invite an illustrator to talk to the class. (Look for freelance artists, newspaper designers, art teachers, or other local resources.) Have him or her share the stages a piece of artwork might go through, from a thumbnail sketch to a final illustration. Especially focus on the process of revising an illustration, and encourage children to draw parallels between this and revising their writing.

Making a Cover/Binding

You Will Need

- several trade books, some familiar to children
- children's final drafts, ready for publishing
- cover stock or construction paper
- book binding supplies such as a stapler, hole punch, yarn

Lesson Background

The writing process becomes more meaningful when children know that they are writing for an audience and that their work will be "published." Classroom publishing includes making a cover and binding the pages together in some fashion.

Teaching the Lesson

1. Display several trade books that are familiar to children. Discuss the book covers and how they relate to the story or content. Ask children why they think books have covers. After listening to their responses, help them conclude that the cover is the first part of the book we see. It is designed to get our attention, to make us want to open and read the book. Point out that the cover includes the book's title and names of the author and illustrator.

2. Explain that children will be designing covers for their own finished work. Ask children to think of several ideas for cover illustrations before settling on what to draw. Remind them that the cover should attract readers and give them an idea of what the book is about.

3. Once children have decided on their cover illustrations, they can visit the bookbinding center to gather paper and art supplies. Have them each design and illustrate a cover, including the title of the book and their own name as author and illustrator.

4. When children have completed their covers, help them bind the cover and pages of their final version along the left-hand edge or top. Use a simple binding technique such as stapling along one edge or punching holes and threading yarn through them.

Teacher Tip

When children brainstorm possible covers for their books, they are also indentifying the main ideas and main characters in their stories. Encourage children to think in these terms as they develop their covers.

Revisiting the Lesson

Always discuss a book's cover before reading it aloud. Ask children if the cover makes them want to read the book. What does it tell them about the book? Following a read-aloud, you may wish to return to the cover to confirm predictions or question elements on it.

Assessment Connection

As children illustrate their book covers, note things such as whether the title is interesting and creative and if the cover illustration reveals something about the subject of the book.

Author's Chair

Lesson Background

When children write for an audience, they add purpose to the writing process. We must, therefore, be certain to provide opportunities for children to share their work with an audience if they desire.

Teaching the Lesson

1. Read aloud the selected trade book. Then ask children why the author may have written and published the story. Lead children to conclude that authors typically want their work published so their stories may be shared with others. Explain that as children become authors, they too will have opportunities to share their work.

2. Present the idea of an Author's Chair, explaining that this is a special place to sit while an author shares his or her work with an audience. You may already have a special chair designated for this purpose. If so, introduce this as the Author's Chair. If not, allow children to help decide which chair will be used for this purpose. You may want to create a sign for the chair.

3. As a group, brainstorm a list of guidelines that authors should follow while using the Author's Chair. Must he or she only read aloud or is it acceptable to simply talk about the story? Should the author share his or her illustrations? Should the author allow time for questions? Should the author practice the reading before sharing it? Can the Author's Chair be used with small groups? Must authors sign up to use the Author's Chair? You may also wish to establish guidelines for the behavior of the audience. May children ask questions during a reading? Is discussion allowed when a person is reading?

4. Display the guidelines near the Author's Chair. Then, sitting in the Author's Chair, read your story and model how an author should share his or her work. Following the reading, discuss audience behavior, explaining how good listeners help to enrich the experience.

5. If you want children to sign up to use the Author's Chair, post a sign-up sheet. Let those who are ready to share sign up and read their books to the class.

Revisiting the Lesson

Modify the Author's Chair guidelines as needed. Encourage children who seem reluctant to use the Author's Chair to begin by sharing their work with one or two peers. Then suggest that they try the Author's Chair if they would like.

You Will Need

- a trade book to read aloud for enjoyment
- a chair, preferably different from the chairs used by children
- chart paper
- marker
- a brief story previously written by you

Sharing Your Work at Home

Teacher Tip

You may find it helpful to communicate with families before sending children home with their work. Offer tips such as these:

- Give your child undivided attention while he or she reads to you.
- Ask relevant questions while avoiding criticism.
- Encourage siblings to listen and add positive feedback.
- Your child may enjoy sharing his or her work over the telephone with a grandparent or other supportive relative.
- Acknowledge the amount of work that went into this final piece.
- Ask about the writing process.
- When your child has finished, help determine a safe, special place to keep the writing.

Lesson Background

Reminding children that their writing will be shared with others adds purpose to the entire writing process. A classroom Author's Chair provides a forum for young writers to share with an audience of their peers. Many children, however, are especially pleased when they are encouraged to take their writing home to share with family members.

Teaching the Lesson

1. As children are involved in the writing process, they should be made aware that their work will be shared with an audience. You may want to teach this lesson when everyone (or almost everyone) is ready to take a completed piece of writing home. Enthusiastically announce that this is an exciting day because they will be taking home a published piece of their writing to share with family members. Explain that because this is so special, you want to be certain they are prepared.

2. Model how to read with expression, paying attention to punctuation and speaking clearly. Help each child find a partner, and instruct the pairs to take turns reading their work to each other. Time permitting, encourage volunteers to sit in the Author's Chair and read to their classmates as they will read to family members.

3. Provide children with construction paper or folders and a variety of art supplies. Have them create and decorate take-home writing folders. Explain that these folders will protect their work as it goes to and from school. You may want to have children add a "comments" page at the back of the folder. Explain that after reading their work, children may ask family members to write comments on this page. Later, they may want to share the comments with the class.

Revisiting the Lesson

Invite parents and other visitors to an Author's Tea or Celebrate Writing Day. Children may wish to take turns describing the writing process to the visitors. Alternatively, writing process information stations (one for editing, another for finding ideas, etc.), led by children, could be arranged. Children may also share their individual writing folders with the visitors.

Self-Assessment (Pictorial)

Lesson Background

As children write, we want them to think about the quality of their writing rather than just the quantity. It is important to model the process of self-reflection. This pictorial assessment will allow children to be reflective while using a form accessible to both readers and nonreaders.

How Did I Do?

I think my story is . . .

I think my pictures are . . .

I want to share my story with . . .

You Will Need

- overhead and transparency
- overhead marker
- a story you have written

Create a transparency of a pictorial self-assessment form to share with children. You may want to create one similar to the design shown at the left. Display your own story on chart paper.

Teaching the Lesson

1. Display the writing self-assessment form. Tell children that when authors finish their writing, they ask themselves if they feel good about their work and if they want to share it with others. They decide if their writing is the best it can be or if they want to do some things differently on the next story they write.

2. Read aloud the story you wrote on chart paper. Then display the pictorial self-assessment form. Explain to children that the form is a helpful way to think about your story. Fill out the self-assessment form on the overhead. Explain your answers out loud so children hear your thought processes.

3. Ask children to complete a pictorial self-assessment form when they finish a story. Explain that they may share this form with a classmate, or with you or keep it to themselves. If you have a central location for blank forms, or a system for filing completed forms with their writing, share this with the class.

Assessment Connection

When conferencing with children, discuss their self-assessments to determine the thought processes used in making their evaluations. Guide children in making accurate, honest assessments—neither too self-critical nor too accepting of low standards.

Revisiting the Lesson

Ask for volunteers to share one of their self-assessment forms and explain why they finished the sentences the way they did.

Self-Assessment (Text)

You Will Need

- a story you have written on chart paper
- the following sentences written on chart paper: I think my story is _____ because..., I think my pictures are _____ because..., I want to share my story with....

Assessment Connection

Note patterns you see over time with self-assessment forms. Areas where children seem uncomfortable can provide you with teaching points. What children hope to do better will also provide teaching points for helping them become better writers.

Lesson Background

As children develop throughout the year as readers and writers, you may want to offer this assessment form to them rather than the form discussed in the previous mini-lesson. As you model your reflections on a story you've written, children will begin to understand how they can reflect on their own writing.

How Did I Do?

I think my story is _____ because . . .

I think my pictures are _____ because . . .

I want to share my story with _____ .

Teaching the Lesson

When writers finish their stories, they think about what they have written to make sure that their writing is the best that it can be before they say it is finished.

I'm going to read my story to you. As I read it, I will be thinking about the things I like in my story. When I finish reading it, I am going to finish these three sentences that I have written here: "I think my story is _____ because..., I think my pictures are _____ because..., and I want to share my story with _____ ."

After reading your story to children, finish the phrases listed above. Model how you would write, including invented spelling. Be sure to think aloud so children can hear your thought processes.

Now I want you to think about a story you have written. You can do the same thing I did, writing down your thoughts about your story. I have sheets for you that I will keep in the writing center *(or wherever you choose)*. Fill the sheet out and keep it with your story. *You will need to develop an organizational system for this.* Remember, these thoughts will help you think about your writing and learn how to become a better writer.

Revisiting the Lesson

Ask for volunteers to share one of their self-assessment forms and explain why they finished the phrases the way they did.

Keeping Track of What You've Written

Lesson Background

Celebrate classroom authors by recording their writing efforts on a chart titled "We Are Authors." Doing so will validate children as authors and help you keep track of their work.

Teaching the Lesson

1. Display the chart for children to see. Explain that as authors they will be doing a lot of writing. They will be writing stories, poems, lists, reports, and many other kinds of work. The chart will help them keep track of what they write. (At this time, explain which kinds of writing you want recorded on the chart.)

2. Model the use of the chart by asking a volunteer to bring up a piece of writing he or she has already done. Help the child record the appropriate information on the chart.

3. Give children individual copies of the chart to keep in their writing folders. Explain that they may keep their own lists of writing as well. On their individual lists, they can record any writing they do, not just the kinds of writing you want on the classroom chart. You may want to ask children to include the date for each piece of writing as well.

Revisiting the Lesson

Throughout the year, reinforce the value of the classroom chart by using it to celebrate children as authors. Occasionally ask children to volunteer to share a piece of writing they have listed on the chart. Discuss what kind of writing the shared piece is.

You Will Need

- chart paper titled "We Are Authors," set up as indicated below
- markers
- 8 1/2" x 11" copies of chart, one per child

Name	Title

Assessment Connection

Use the "We Are Authors" chart as a helpful tool to assess the variety of writing subjects and genres being used by children in their writing.

Writing Checklist

Name: _____

Date: _____

Grade: _____

Age: _____

Applications	*Sometimes*	*Always*	*Never*
• Uses labels and captions in writing			
• Retells personal experiences			
• Writes narratives based on personal experiences			
• Writes narratives			
• Writes letters (informal, formal)			
• Writes descriptions			
• Demonstrates understanding of expository forms			
• Demonstrates an awareness of story structure (beginning, middle, end)			
Organization and Focus			
• Writes to communicate ideas and reflections			
• Selects writing forms for specific purposes and audiences			
• Maintains a central idea or single focus			
• Presents information in a logical sequence			
• Uses knowledge of regular spelling patterns (CVC; CVCe)			
• Uses basic capitalization and punctuation rules			

Writing Checklist (continued)

Name: _____

Date: _____

Grade: _____

Age: _____

	Sometimes	Always	Never
Organization and Focus (continued)			
• Writes messages that move from left to right and top to bottom			
• Demonstrates an understanding of the alphabetic principle			
• Uses letters and phonetically spelled words			
• Uses conventional spellings for simple, regularly spelled words			
• Connects related ideas in writing			
Evaluation and Revision			
• Uses a variety of prewriting strategies			
• Uses a variety of revising strategies			
• Revises selected drafts to include more descriptive and sensory details			
• Uses a variety of reference materials to revise			
Sentence Structure and Grammar			
• Uses basic capitalization and punctuation rules			
• Uses complete sentences and recognizes correct word order			
• Uses singular and plural nouns correctly in writing			
Penmanship			
• Writes uppercase and lowercase letters of the alphabet			
• Writes clearly and legibly			
• Allows adequate spacing between letters, words, and sentences			

A Bibliography of Professional Resources

Craft Lessons: Teaching Writing K–8 by Ralph Fletcher and Joann Portalupi, Stenhouse Publishers, 1998. The authors present organized writing lessons to support teachers as they work with children who craft their own writing pieces.

Creating Classrooms for Authors and Inquirers by Jerome Harste and Kathy Short, Heinemann, 1996. Creating a classroom environment for reading and writing, and establishing an author cycle framework are discussed in this book.

A Fresh Look at Writing by Donald Graves, Heinemann, 1994. Donald Graves presents the latest ideas on teaching writing in a comprehensive resource for new teachers as well as master teachers.

Highlight My Strengths: Assessment and Evaluation of Literacy Learning by Leanna Traill, Rigby, 1995. This handbook for assessment and evaluation includes the detailed stages of literacy development and a variety of assessment tools.

Ideas for Spelling by Faye Bolton and Diane Snowball, Heinemann, 1993. Detailed strategies and activities within the reading and writing curriculum are provided for helping children at all stages of spelling development.

Invitations: Changing as Teachers and Learners K–12 by Regie Routman, Heinemann, 1994. Regie Routman invites all teachers to reflect upon their own practice and provides in-depth information with step-by-step demonstration lessons for teaching writing.

Lasting Impressions: Weaving Literature into the Writing Workshop by Shelley Harwayne, Heinemann, 1992. Shelley Harwayne, a New York City principal, shares stories of real children and her own love of literature as she reexamines the structure and dynamics of the writing workshop.

Living Between the Lines by Lucy Calkins, Heinemann, 1990.
Lucy Calkins' presentation of the reading-writing workshop details the use of writers' notebooks to establish real-life reading and writing connections.

What a Writer Needs by Ralph Fletcher, Heinemann, 1993. Ralph Fletcher focuses on helping children improve as writers by providing specific practical strategies for challenging and extending children's writing.

Writing: Teachers and Children at Work by Donald Graves, Heinemann, 1983. This Donald Graves classic describes the learning theory and classroom practice of the writing workshop.